"PROVOCATIVE, PRACTICAL, POWERFUL!"

Stephen R. Covey
Author of The 7 Habits of Highly Effective People

"For any executive this is an excellent roadmap for leading strategic change!"

J. W. Marriott, Jr.
Chairman and CEO, Marriott International, Inc.

"Few things add greater value than effectively leading strategic change. Few books show you how to do it better than this one."

David Ulrich
Author of The HR Scorecard *and named* BusinessWeek's *#1 Business Guru*

"*Leading Strategic Change* is a must-read guidebook for leaders in any business organization. Black and Gregersen not only identify common barriers to success, they also provide a framework for breaking old habits, mapping new paths, and setting a course for effective change."

Kevin Rollins
Vice Chairman of the Board and COO, Dell Computer Corporation

"Before cracking the cover on *Leading Strategic Change*, I couldn't imagine how another book on change could deliver anything new to a CEO. Surprise! I was astonished by how rapidly Black and Gregersen broke through my brain barrier. They deliver a fascinating perspective and practical toolkit to deliver faster strategic change in our growing, global company."

Thomas Grimm
CEO and President, Sam's Club, and Executive Vice President, Wal-Mart

"Black and Gregersen debunk the myth that organizations change by changing the organization. They understand the real dynamics a leader must manage to convert the hearts and minds of people in a complex organization to a new direction. If you are trying to shake things up and make lasting change, this is the book you must read."

Gary L. Crittenden
CFO, American Express

"Finally a book on change that gets it right. Organizations don't change. People change. Black and Gregersen give the reader extremely practical tools to make real change happen."

Jack Zenger
Vice Chairman of Provant and co-author of The Extraordinary Leader

"I have been provoked to look at my business in a different light by the concepts developed by Black and Gregersen. The 'brain barriers' that they describe are a very real threat to any business that hopes to compete in this fast changing environment."

James H. Nuckols
CEO, The Sporting News

"This book broke my own brain barrier, asking me to think differently about ideas and processes that I'd become too comfortable with. It's a significant contribution to the field of organizational change and will undoubtedly help us be more successful with change. And I love the maps—they provoke my intellect and imagination."

Margaret J. Wheatley
Author of Leadership and the New Science *and* Turning to One Another

"A significant barrier to any major change or innovation management process is in transparently defining the past and desired future state, then connecting the move from former to latter in an inspirational way. *Leading Strategic Change* offers novel framing and straightforward step-back, targeted thinking that can streamline and turbocharge the challenging change progress."

David N. DiGiulio
Vice President, Research & Development, Procter & Gamble

"Leading successful strategic change is one of the biggest and most important challenges executives face today. Black and Gregersen offer a practical set of concepts and tools to meet that challenge."

Sue Lee
Senior Vice President Human Resources & Communications, Suncor Energy Inc.

"I found this book special in several ways. It is not the usual description of the stages of change. Instead, it describes the process of change in human terms—the way people really experience it. They go beneath and look at the assumptions (mind maps) that hold people back from being able to change."

Jean Broom
Senior Vice President, Human Resources, Itochu International, Inc.

"Talk about change has far outstripped leaders' ability to successfully lead it. Black and Gregersen push the change leaders to explore how they think about or 'map' the world in which we live. These maps become either a critical barrier or an asset to their ability to lead change. The authors also provide a challenging self-examination for the serious leader to assess his or her ability to create long-lasting and effective change. Thoughtful leaders will give this a very thoughtful read."

Ralph Christensen
Senior Vice President, Human Resources, Hallmark Cards, Inc.

"Strategic change happens one person at a time. Black and Gregersen bring this statement to life by supplying critical insight combined with essential tools for helping individuals negotiate their way through organizational change."

Tyler Bolli
Manager, Human Resources, Kohler Company

"This book presents a refreshing new way to think about leading change in organizations. Black and Gregersen redraw our maps of the change process in a compelling and practical way that gets right to the heart of making real change possible."

Marion Shumway
Organization Development Manager, Intel Corporation

"Insightful handbook packed full of valuable wisdom for unlocking the power of mental maps in any organization's change efforts."

Dave Kinard
Director of Organizational Effectiveness, Eli Lilly and Company

"What a pleasure to find a book on change focused on 'leading' rather than 'managing' change. Leaders *create* change; they don't react to it. This book addresses the crux of that leadership issue by focusing on people, where the real change must occur."

Richard D. Hanks
CEO, BlueStep, Inc.

"Too often in the trenches of organizational life, we deceive ourselves by believing that if we get the boxes in an organization chart or the big systems behind the boxes just right, then organizations change. Black and Gregersen artfully uncover this deception by revealing a new, eye-opening approach to change that can help any leader of change become much stronger and better at it."

Mark Hamberlin
Senior Finance Manager, Cisco Systems Inc.

About *Leading Strategic Change*

Today, virtually every organization faces massive change. Unfortunately, change is extraordinarily difficult and most attempts to initiate and implement change fail. In *Leading Strategic Change*, J. Stewart Black and Hal B. Gregersen identify the core problem: changing the "mental maps" inside each of our heads.

Just as actual maps guide people's footsteps, mental maps guide daily behavior. Successful strategic change for the organization is all about changing individuals first, because they are the organization.

To change organizations, you must break through the brain barrier. Perhaps Yogi Berra described it best when he claimed, "Ninety percent of baseball is mental. The other fifty percent is physical." So, too, in business.

Leading Strategic Change systematically shows how to make the most important change of all: "redrawing" individuals' mental maps with new destinations and paths. Black and Gregersen identify the brain barriers that keep strategic change from success: failure to see, failure to move, and failure to finish.

Overcoming the failure to see
Why organizations miss obvious market transformations—and what to do about it

Breaking through the failure to move
Why people fail to change—even when they see the need—and how to break through this barrier

Conquering the failure to finish
Why change "stalls out" and how to maintain the momentum

Anticipating change
Creating the capability to anticipate change, move when needed, and finish in the future without "being told"

LEADING
Strategic
CHANGE

LEADING
Strategic
CHANGE

Breaking Through the
BRAIN BARRIER

J. STEWART BLACK
HAL B. GREGERSEN

An Imprint of PEARSON EDUCATION
Upper Saddle River, NJ • New York • London • San Francisco • Toronto • Sydney
Tokyo • Singapore • Hong Kong • Cape Town • Madrid
Paris • Milan • Munich • Amsterdam
www.ftpress.com

Library of Congress Cataloging-in-Publication Data
Available Upon Request

Editorial/production supervision: *Patti Guerrieri*
Executive editor: *Tim Moore*
Editorial assistant: *Allyson Kloss*
Development editor: *Russ Hall*
Marketing manager: *Alexis R. Heydt-Long*
Manufacturing buyer: *Maura Zaldivar*
Cover design director: *Jerry Votta*
Cover design: *Talar Boorujy*
Art director: *Gail Cocker-Bogusz*
Interior design: *Meg Van Arsdale*

© 2003 Pearson Education, Inc.
Publishing as FT Press
Upper Saddle River, New Jersey 07458

FT Press books are widely used by corporations and
government agencies for training, marketing, and resale.

For information regarding corporate and government bulk discounts
please contact: Corporate and Government Sales (800) 382-3419 or
corpsales@pearsontechgroup.com
Or write: Prentice Hall PTR, Corporate Sales Dept., One Lake Street,
Upper Saddle River, NJ 07458.

Printed in the United States of America

Eighth Printing

ISBN 0-13-130319-8

Pearson Education LTD.
Pearson Education Australia PTY, Limited
Pearson Education Singapore, Pte. Ltd.
Pearson Education North Asia Ltd.
Pearson Education Canada, Ltd.
Pearson Educación de Mexico, S.A. de C.V.
Pearson Education—Japan
Pearson Education Malaysia, Pte. Ltd.

F T Press Books

For more information, please go to www.ftpress.com

Business and Society

John Gantz and Jack B. Rochester
  Pirates of the Digital Millennium: How the Intellectual Property Wars Damage Our Personal Freedoms, Our Jobs, and the World Economy

Douglas K. Smith
  On Value and Values: Thinking Differently About We in an Age of Me

Current Events

Alan Elsner
  Gates of Injustice: The Crisis in America's Prisons

John R. Talbott
  Where America Went Wrong: And How to Regain Her Democratic Ideals

Economics

David Dranove
  What's Your Life Worth? Health Care Rationing…Who Lives? Who Dies? Who Decides?

Entrepreneurship

Dr. Candida Brush, Dr. Nancy M. Carter, Dr. Elizabeth Gatewood,
Dr. Patricia G. Greene, and Dr. Myra M. Hart
  Clearing the Hurdles: Women Building High Growth Businesses

Oren Fuerst and Uri Geiger
  From Concept to Wall Street: A Complete Guide to Entrepreneurship and Venture Capital

David Gladstone and Laura Gladstone
  Venture Capital Handbook: An Entrepreneur's Guide to Raising Venture Capital, Revised and Updated

Thomas K. McKnight
  Will It Fly? How to Know if Your New Business Idea Has Wings… Before You Take the Leap

Stephen Spinelli, Jr., Robert M. Rosenberg, and Sue Birley
  Franchising: Pathway to Wealth Creation

Executive Skills

Cyndi Maxey and Jill Bremer
  It's Your Move: Dealing Yourself the Best Cards in Life and Work

Richard W. Paul and Linda Elder
  Critical Thinking

John Putzier
  Weirdos in the Workplace

Finance

Aswath Damodaran
  The Dark Side of Valuation: Valuing Old Tech, New Tech, and New Economy Companies

Kenneth R. Ferris and Barbara S. Pécherot Petitt
  Valuation: Avoiding the Winner's Curse

International Business and Globalization

Robert A. Isaak
The Globalization Gap: How the Rich Get Richer and the Poor Get Left Further Behind

Peter Marber
Money Changes Everything: How Global Prosperity Is Reshaping Our Needs, Values, and Lifestyles

Fernando Robles, Françoise Simon, and Jerry Haar
Winning Strategies for the New Latin Markets

Investments

Gerald Appel
Technical Analysis: Power Tools for Active Investors

Victor Canto
Understanding Asset Allocation: An Intuitive Approach to Maximizing Your Portfolio

Guy Cohen
The Bible of Options Strategies: The Definitive Guide for Practical Trading Strategies

Guy Cohen
Options Made Easy, Second Edition: Your Guide to Profitable Trading

Michael Covel
Trend Following: How Great Traders Make Millions in Up or Down Markets

Aswath Damodaran
Investment Fables: Exposing the Myths of "Can't Miss" Investment Strategies

Harry Domash
Fire Your Stock Analyst! Analyzing Stocks on Your Own

David Gladstone and Laura Gladstone
Venture Capital Investing: The Complete Handbook for Investing in Businesses for Outstanding Profits

Michael N. Kahn
Technical Analysis Plain and Simple, Second Edition: Charting the Markets in Your Language

Charles D. Kirkpatrick and Julie R. Dahlquist
Technical Analysis: The Complete Resource for Financial Market Technicians

George Kleinman
Trading Commodities and Financial Futures, Third Edition

Yiannis G. Mostrous, Elliott H. Gue, and Ivan D. Martchev
The Silk Road to Riches: How You Can Profit by Investing in Asia's Newfound Prosperity

W. Edward Olmstead
Options for the Beginner and Beyond: Unlock the Opportunities and Minimize the Risks

Peter Rosenstreich
Forex Revolution: An Insider's Guide to the Real World of Foreign Exchange Trading

Michael C. Thomsett
Options Trading for the Conservative Investor

Michael Thomsett
Stock Profits: Getting to the Core—New Fundamentals for a New Age

Marketing

David Arnold
The Mirage of Global Markets: How Globalizing Companies Can Succeed as Markets Localize

Michael Basch
CustomerCulture: How FedEx and Other Great Companies Put the Customer First Every Day

Deirdre Breakenridge and Thomas J. DeLoughry
The New PR Toolkit

Jonathan Cagan and Craig M. Vogel
Creating Breakthrough Products: Innovation from Product Planning to Program Approval

Lewis P. Carbone
Clued In: How To Keep Customers Coming Back Again And Again

Bernd H. Schmitt, David L. Rogers, and Karen Vrotsos
There's No Business That's Not Show Business: Marketing in Today's Experience Culture

Yoram J. Wind and Vijay Mahajan, with Robert Gunther
Convergence Marketing: Strategies for Reaching the New Hybrid Consumer

Personal Finance

David Shapiro
Retirement Countdown: Take Action Now to Get the Life You Want

Lois A. Vitt
10 Secrets to Successful Home Buying and Selling: Using Your Housing Psychology to Make Smarter Decisions

Steve Weisman
50 Ways to Protect Your Identity and Your Credit: Everything You Need to Know About Identity Theft, Credit Cards, Credit Repair, and Credit Reports

Steve Weisman
Boomer or Bust: Your Financial Guide to Retirement, Health Care, Medicare, and Long-Term Care

Steve Weisman
A Guide to Elder Planning: Everything You Need to Know to Protect Yourself Legally and Financially

Liz Pulliam Weston
Deal with Your Debt: The Right Way to Manage Your Bills and Pay Off What You Owe

Liz Pulliam Weston
Your Credit Score: How to Fix, Improve, and Protect the 3-Digit Number That Shapes Your Financial Future

Strategy

Edward W. Davis and Robert E. Spekmam
The Extended Enterprise: Gaining Competitive Advantage through Collaborative Supply Chains

Nicholas D. Evans
Business Innovation and Disruptive Technology

Stacy Perman
Spies, Inc.

Joel M. Shulman, With Thomas T. Stallkamp
Getting Bigger by Growing Smaller: A New Growth Model for Corporate America

CONTENTS

Foreword

Theories are predictive statements of what causes what, and why. Many managers view themselves as practical men and women and don't view their actions as being guided by theory. But every plan that a manager makes and every action that a manager takes are, in fact, predicated on some theory in his or her mind—a belief that certain events or actions will result in particular outcomes. "If we cut price, more people will buy more" is an action predicated on a theory. "If I give her a performance-based financial incentive, she will work harder and more productively" is another. "If I out source this subsystem to a supplier that does the job more cost-effectively than we can do it in-house, we'll be more competitive" is a third. These theories serve as mental maps guiding the everyday actions managers take.

Too often, though, managers aren't even aware of these powerful mental maps—beliefs about cause and effect—that they employ when making plans and taking actions. Still, the maps are there, somewhere in the managers' minds. Like it or not, every manager is, therefore, a theory-driven manager.

Most theories that managers use were formulated through experience—and because members of management teams experience many things in common, they end up employing similar theories, consciously or unconsciously, as they make decisions. Edgar Schein, Massachusetts Institute of Technology's noted scholar of organizations, has shown how these shared theories develop and come to comprise an organization's culture.[1] He notes that, in the earliest days of every organization's history, there came a point when a group of people had to get something done. Confronted with that task, they put their heads together and figured out how they would approach the challenge. If their efforts failed, then the next time that task arose, they would be inclined to devise another way to get the job done. If that method proved successful, then the next time the task arose, the group would be inclined to use the same method to get the job done. If that method proved successful again when the same task arose, they would be even *more* likely to address the task with the same approach when it arose again, and so on.

Ultimately, if a group of people have successfully worked together in particular ways to address recurrent tasks again and again, they come simply to assume that this is the way they should do things. When this happens—when people begin adopting ways of working by assumption, rather than by explicit debate and decision—that process becomes part of the organization's culture. This is what an organization's culture is: ways of getting things done that a group of people have used so successfully for so long that they simply come to assume that doing things the same way is the only way to get the needed result. As a consequence, the more successful the organization is, the stronger will this unconscious consensus about cause and effect become. Another way to put it is that, because theories are statements of what causes what and why, an organization's culture is actually a collection of theories in use. These theories provide valuable guidance to managers as they make plans and take actions, because they build on what individuals in the organization have learned from their collective experience. In fact, orga-

---

1.   *Schein, Edgar, *Organizational Culture and Leadership*, 2d. San Francisco: Jossey-Bass Publishers, 1997.

nizations with strong cultures or theories in use become in many ways self-managing, because managers in disparate parts of the company can be trusted to make decisions autonomously that are consistent with what the company has learned will work.

All of this is good, of course, except when things change. Then the widely shared maps that managers have unconsciously used to predict what events and actions will produce the needed results may no longer hold true. This is why I'm delighted that Stewart and Hal have written this book. In its pages, they present methods for discovering the implicit theories in-use that managers have learned to trust in the course of building successful companies—theories that must be understood explicitly before new ones can be adopted in times of change.

No panaceas address any or all of the problems of management completely. I certainly hope that no one who reads this book has bought it to find an easy answer to the problems of managing change. But I do believe that when a talented group of managers can share a common language and a common way to frame the origin of the problems they face, they can do remarkable things. And I believe that *Leading Strategic Change* delivers essential methods that managers can employ to encourage these vital efforts.

Clayton M. Christensen
Robert & Jane Cizik Professor of Business Administration
Harvard Business School

ACKNOWLEDGMENTS

Over twenty years ago, J. Bonner Ritchie rewrote the maps in each of our minds. As students, he confronted us with unsettling contrasts to our worldviews. Bonner had a level of inquisitiveness and love of learning greater than either of us had ever experienced before. He was a champion of change whether as a student at the University of California, Berkeley, an officer for the U.S. Army, a faculty member and civil rights activist at the University of Michigan Business School, a business consultant to African American catfish farmers, a chairperson of the Utah State Liquor Commission, or currently as a tireless advocate of peace and prosperity for children around the world.

Bonner also infused us with a conviction about the power of maps and metaphors, and instilled an understanding of how looking at the world through maps or metaphors can help us see the things more clearly. For the gift of maps and the insight of metaphor, we thank Bonner.

Along with Bonner, many other colleagues such as Jean Broom, Gordon Finch, Mark Hamberlin, Allen Morrison, Mark Mendenhall, Gary Oddou, Paul McKinnon, Lee Perry, Lyman Porter, Kurt Sandholtz, Marion Shumway, Greg Stewart, Pat Stocker, Dave Ulrich, and Dave Whetten have helped shape our maps about the challenges and opportunities of change. In addition, thousands of executive education participants as well as graduate students at the University of Michigan, Brigham Young University, Dartmouth College, Helsinki School of Economics, Penn State University, and Thunderbird have engaged in learning with us as we worked over the years to sharpen our understanding of mental maps and their decisive impacts on change initiatives.

On the home front, our respective parents played pivotal roles in not only forming our maps of the world, but also teaching us how to create new maps. We are grateful for the gifts of inquiry that parents passed on. We also thank each of our children—Jared, Nathaniel, Kendra, Ian, and Devyn Black as well as Matt, Ryan, and Amber Gregersen—for enduring our quirky mental maps for years and working overtime to rewrite and update some of the tired and well-worn ones that needed changing. Finally, we dedicate this book to our wives—Tanya Black and Ann Gregersen. We are ever grateful for the map of life that we share individually with each of them.

J. Stewart Black
Hal B. Gregersen

About the Authors

J. Stewart Black, Ph.D. is a professor of business administration at the University of Michigan. An internationally recognized scholar on change and transformation, he is a frequent keynote speaker at conferences around the world and company functions. He is regularly sought out to help leading companies globally with strategic change initiatives and the development of their senior leaders and high potential managers. Dr. Black has served on the faculties of the Amos Tuck School of Business Administration at Dartmouth College and the University of California, Irvine. He is the author of eight other books and nearly 100 articles and case studies that have been widely used in both university classrooms and corporate boardrooms.

Hal B. Gregersen is the Donald L. Staheli Professor of Global Leadership in the Marriott School at Brigham Young University and taught previously at Dartmouth College, Pennsylvania State University, and the Turku School of Economics in Finland as a Fulbright Fellow. Dr. Gregersen is a frequent keynote conference speaker on leading strategic change and an executive education contributor in companies (Cemex, IBM, Intel, LG Group, Lockheed Martin, Marriott, and Nokia) and universities (University of Michigan, Helsinki School of Economics, Tufts University, Thunderbird, and University of Western Ontario) around the world. As author of seven books and over 60 articles in publications like the *Harvard Business Review* and *Sloan Management Review*, Dr. Gregersen is a globally respected scholar on how firms find and build executive leaders capable of conceiving and achieving worldwide change. He has appeared on programs such as *CNNfn* and his cutting-edge research on global leadership has been cited in numerous publications such as *BusinessWeek*, *Fortune*, and *The Wall Street Journal*.

1

THE CHALLENGE OF LEADING STRATEGIC CHANGE

With over a hundred books on leading strategic change to choose from, why read this one? The answer is simple. Most other books on change have it backward. They take an "organization in" approach; in other words, they outline all the organizational levers you should pull to change the company so that individual change will follow. Our experience and research commands the opposite conclusion. Lasting success lies in changing individuals first; then the organization follows. An organization changes only as far or as fast as its collective individuals change. Consequently, instead of an "organization in" approach, we take an "individual out" approach. To repeat—to strategically change your organization, you must *first* change individuals.

Unlocking individual change starts and ends with the mental maps people carry in their heads—how they see the organization and their jobs. Just as actual maps guide the steps people take on a hike through the Himalayas, mental maps direct people's behavior in daily organizational life. And if leaders cannot change individual's mental maps, they will not change the destinations people pursue or the paths they take to get there. As a result, successful strategic change requires a focus on individuals and redrawing their mental maps. If what is in people's heads is not remapped, if you cannot break through this "brain barrier," their hearts and hands have nothing new to follow. As a result, leading strategic change requires becoming an effective mental cartographer, or Map Maker.

Perfecting this capability is probably one of the most profitable things you can do for your career and for your company. In our research, just over 80% of companies listed leading change as one of the top five core leadership competencies for the future. Perhaps more importantly, 85% felt that this competency was not as strong as was needed within their high-potential leaders. In a nutshell, when it comes to leading strategic change, demand is high (and growing), and supply is short.

To understand why a shortage of capable leaders of change persists, we need to consider only a few factors. First, change has never been easy. For example, consider this quote written 500 years ago by Niccolo Machiavelli:

> There is nothing more difficult to carry out, nor more doubtful of success, nor more dangerous to handle than to initiate a new order of things. For the reformer has enemies in all those who profit by the old order, and only lukewarm defenders by all those who could profit by the new order. This lukewarmness arises from the incredulity of mankind who *do not truly believe in anything new until they have had actual experience with it.*

Clearly, resistance to change is not a modern concept. In fact, resistance to change seems to have endured through the ages, in part because humans are biologically hard-wired to resist change. Yes, that's right. We are programmed *not* to change. Although plants may evolve and survive through random variation and natural selection, people do not. We do not generate random variations in behavior and let nature take its course—selecting and deselecting those who fit and do not fit the environment. We are wired to resist random change and, thereby, avoid random deselection. We are wired to survive, so we hang on to what has worked in the past.

This map-hugging dynamic happened to Hal a few years ago, when he was teaching in the Amos Tuck School of Business at Dartmouth College. Even though Hal lived only about a mile from work and had several possible ways to get there, he had quickly settled in on a habitual driving route that took him to work quickest. One cold winter morning, though, Hal had driven about halfway to work when he confronted a detour barricade and sign. Construction workers were laying new pipe under the road, so Hal had to turn around, backtrack halfway home, and follow a detour route to work. At the end of the workday, Hal started his short drive home. But again, he took his "usual" route and ended up stuck at the detour sign once more. He backed up (just like he did in the morning) and ultimately rerouted himself home. The next day, Hal woke up and hurried off to work and—you guessed it—Hal's a slow learner. He took his "usual" route again and ended up staring once more at the detour sign. Like the day before, he turned around, backtracked, followed the detour route, and made it to work. Finally, on the afternoon of the second day, Hal started to alter his mental map of how to drive home and actually rerouted himself *before* running into the detour sign.

Unfortunately, modern times conspire against this ancient biological code of hanging on ferociously to what works until undeniable evidence mounts against our map that it no longer fits the environment. For example, the rate and magnitude of required change has grown exponentially. We now talk about 90-day years (i.e., Internet years, which are almost as short as dog years.) Pundits pull out charts that show the half-life of products dropping in half. In fact, many of us face change of such enormous scope, size, and complexity that it is nearly overwhelming:

- transforming a business unit that succeeded for years by focusing on technological prowess to a unit that must now focus on customer service,

- leading an organization from domestic competition to the global battlefield,

- accelerating growth by focusing not just on building things but on all the services that go with after-sales support,

- changing the culture from one of considered deliberations to a fast, first-mover approach,

- redesigning jobs to incorporate new technology that we hardly understand, or

- something else just as daunting.

Bottom line, the pace, size, and complexity of change are greater than ever before. Consequently, the costs of changing late are not just inconvenient but often catastrophic.

We don't need to look far to see the consequences of not meeting this challenge. Xerox, Lucent, and Kmart in the United States, De Beers in Europe, and Mitsubishi in Japan are just a few examples of companies that faltered, brought in new leaders to champion change, and still failed to recover. Beyond these visible company examples are literally thousands of invisible individual examples—middle-level leaders whose seemingly fast-track careers derailed when a change initiative they were leading crashed and burned.

Although likely frustrating, the fact of the matter is that, no matter how good we have been at leading change in the past, the future will demand even more of us—especially because people are programmed to resist any effort to redraw their mental maps and walk in new paths. The mental terrain of their brains poses a significant set of barriers that we must break through to meet the increasing demands of leading strategic change.

THE CRUX OF THE CHALLENGE

This brings us to the crux of the challenge. Clearly, change has always been and remains difficult. Unless we can dig beneath the surface and expose the fundamentals of why this is so, we have no hope or prayer of meeting these ever-escalating demands on leaders of change.

To better understand these fundamentals, we might take a page from the fundamentals of flight. Breaking the bonds of earth and soaring above the clouds has never been easy. Gravity has been a natural, fundamental force in keeping us down from the beginning. Flight requires thrust, lift, and aerodynamics. We must

EXHIBIT 1-1
F/A-18 Hornet jet breaking through the sound barrier. (Photo John Gay/©AFP/CORBIS)

master these key factors to overcome gravity and break through the barriers of resistance.

Take a moment to study the picture in Exhibit 1-1. This incredible photo captures an F/A-18 Hornet fighter jet hitting Mach I, the speed of sound.

When approaching Mach I, powerful but usually invisible sound waves bunch tighter and tighter together, forming a massive wall of energy that tries to buffet and shake the plane right out of the sky. Without sufficient thrust, lift, and proper aerodynamic design, disaster is inevitable as this sound barrier combines with the forces of gravity to crush the plane and bring it crashing back to earth. Lucky for the pilot of this plane, the designer possessed an in-depth understanding of these fundamentals to achieve breakthrough, letting her punch through the sound barrier as though it were a puff of smoke.

Change in organizations follows the same path. The faster a leader tries to force change, the more shock waves of resistance compact together, forming a massive barrier to success. Instead of a sound barrier though, leaders confront a "brain barrier"

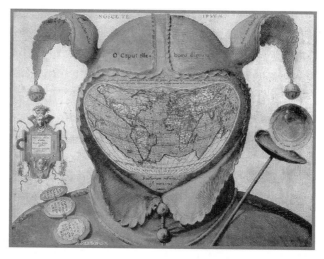

EXHIBIT 1-2
The court jester's mental map. (Fools Map of the World, c. 1590, reference [shelfmark] Douce
Portfolio 142 (92) Bodleian Library, University of Oxford.)

composed of preexisting *and* successful mental maps. These
incredibly powerful maps determine how people see the world of
work, guiding their daily steps and behaviors. Indeed, our heads
are chock full of such maps, and just as the court jester shown in
Exhibit 1-2, the maps in our head—far more than the eyes on
our face—frame our personal views of the world.

The power of these mental maps surprised our colleague several
years ago. He was hired as a consultant to help transform a meat-
packing factory from an authoritarian top-down management
system to a high-involvement, participative one. After three days
of intensive training focused on the opportunities, challenges,
and everyday logistics associated with self-managed work teams,
a burly 300-pound butcher stood up in the back of the room,
slammed a meat cleaver into the table, and demanded in no
uncertain terms that he still had "a right to have a manager tell
me what to do and when to do it." Clearly, this butcher's maps of
his world at work had not budged an inch. And for significant

organizational change to take hold of peoples' hearts and hands in this meat-packing plant—or anywhere else, for that matter—Map Makers of change must comprehend, break through, and ultimately redraw individual mental maps, one by one, person by person, again and again.

The challenge of remapping mental terrain brings us to the critical barriers that prevent sustainable strategic change. What are the natural gravitational forces that suppress change and build brain barriers to breakthroughs? The answer lies in three questions that capture the essence of failed change. And if we can understand why change fails (which it most often does), we can figure out what the necessary thrust, lift, and aerodynamics are for pulling off breakthrough change.

- Why, when opportunities or threats stare people in the face, do people *fail to see* the need to change?

- Even when people see the need, why do they often still *fail to move*?

- Even when people move, why do they *fail to finish*—not going far or fast enough?

If we can grasp why people fail to see, move, and finish, and if we can break through these three barriers, we can deliver strategic change. This book reveals not only how mental maps create these three barriers, but how mental maps also generate the key to breaking through them.

SIMPLIFY AND APPLY

As we explain brain barriers and how to break through them, we try to follow an important principle reflected in the following quote attributed to Albert Einstein: "We should make things as simple as possible, but no simpler." In our view, the eight mistakes, twelve steps, and so on offered by others about change are often correct in direction but overly complicated in reality. But wait—we just got through arguing that today's changes are bigger and more complicated than the past and that changes in the future are likely only to get more daunting. Why would simplifying change help us lead ever more complex changes? There are two reasons.

First, something is practical only if we can remember and recall it. No matter how comprehensive a model, framework, theory, or idea, if we cannot remember and recall it when application is demanded, it ends up making very little practical difference. If change in today's organizations is more prevalent, fast, unexpected, and complex than ever before, it is equally critical for us to act when change is necessary. Whatever tools of change we hope to use well must be remembered, recalled, and applied.

However, long history and scientific evidence teaches us that humans are limited when it comes to remembering and recalling models, frameworks, or even strings of numbers that are too long or complicated. For example, ever wonder why most phone numbers around the world contain only seven digits or less? It is because 80% of the population can remember seven digits, but that percentage drops dramatically as you add digits. In fact, you need to add only three additional digits to those seven, and the percentage of people who can remember them (ten digits versus seven) drops from 80% to only about 2%. If a change strategy sounds great on paper but can't be remembered by people in the field, it really isn't worth anything. For this reason, we take a very pragmatic approach in proposing a framework for leading change. We offer a framework that can be remembered, recalled, and—most importantly—applied.

Second, we argue for simplification because achieving 80% of the desired results rapidly is much better than never attaining 100%. If 80% quickly is your target, then 20% of the factors are the key.

For example, we commonly see cases in which 20% of a firm's customers account for 80% of sales (known as the *80/20 principle*). In sports, we see many situations where 80% of the team's points come from 20% of its players. And although a firm cannot ignore its other customers or a team its full roster of players, both organizations get the best bang for their buck by focusing on the critical core—the fundamentals. For this reason, we focus on the most critical elements of change.

One of the most important differences about *Leading Strategic Change* is that we keep the concepts simple and focus on the fundamentals. We have found through our work with a variety of firms that if you get the change fundamentals right—the critical 20%—the rest comes more easily. Conversely, you can spend truckloads of time on all the fancy frills of change, and ignored fundamentals will steal success away.

In fact, breakthrough change requires a complete mastery of the fundamentals. Just as mastering the fundamentals of gravity and friction allowed designers to narrow the nose and sweep back the wings on planes for pilots to break the sound barrier, mastering change fundamentals delivers the key to breaking through powerful and persistent mental resistance barriers.

THE FUNDAMENTALS OF CHANGE

What are the fundamental dynamics of leading strategic change? The diagram in Exhibit 1-3 attempts to capture this process, and subsequent short sections describe these dynamics relative to each stage of the matrix. And as we mentioned, real mastery of these concepts will come as subsequent chapters walk you through these dynamics in much greater detail.

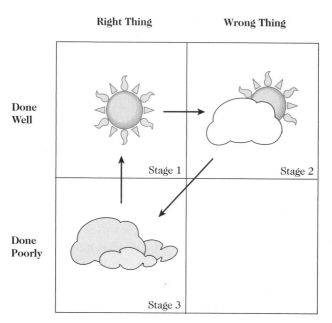

EXHIBIT 1-3
Strategic change matrix.

Virtually every major change has its roots in success (Stage 1). In almost every case, the need for change is born of past success—of doing the right thing and doing it well. The more right it is and the better it has been done, the more likely that it has a long rather than short history. For example, IBM did the right thing (making mainframe computers) and did it well. It did it better than anyone else for nearly 50 years. Xerox was so closely tied to the invention and commercialization of copying that the company name became a verb ("Please Xerox this document for me.")

Change starts with a history of doing the right thing and doing it very well, but then something happens: The environment shifts, and the right thing becomes the wrong thing. A new competitor comes on the scene with equal quality but significantly lower price, or a new technology renders past standards of product reliability obsolete, or government regulations disallow previous business practices, or customers change their preferences, or a million and one other shifts.

As a consequence of the shift, what was once right is now wrong (an initial shift from Stage 1 to Stage 2). And the really frustrating thing is that, although the old right thing is now wrong, we still do it well. In IBM's case, computing power soared while cost remained constant; and servers, minicomputers, and even desktop computers began to replace the role of some mainframes. Just making big boxes was no longer the right thing, but IBM continued doing it so well. People's hearts and souls, their self-worth and image were tied up in years and years of making "big iron" (mainframes in IBM's vernacular). This persistent desire to travel along old, familiar and successful paths of the past is why the first stage of change often results in no change.

However, after enough pain, blood, or at least red ink, we start the second stage of change by finally recognizing that the old right thing is now the wrong thing—we finally see the light. We then begin to envision what the new right thing might be. Over time, the new right thing becomes clear.

But, in almost every case, because the *new* right thing is *new*, we are usually not very good at it at first. Initially, we end up doing the new right thing quite poorly. This challenge forms the third and frustrating stage of change.

For example, not long after Lou Gerstner took over as CEO at IBM, people inside the company finally saw that just "selling boxes" would not work and that providing integrated solutions was critical to their future success. However, neither IBM nor its employees was good at making money from providing integrated solutions at first. Although analysts today tout the importance of "solutions" in IBM's revenue and profit growth, we quickly forget that, back in the early 1990s as IBM initiated this strategic change, the "integrated solution units" (*ISUs,* as they were called) were losing money, not making it.

Hopefully, after a time, we master the new right thing and start to do it well (a move from Stage 3 back to Stage 1). At this point, the sun shines again, and we bask in the warmth of its rays. Life is good. (Well, that is until the new right thing once again becomes the wrong thing.) IBM eventually did become proficient at providing integrated solutions. In fact, the service business was the largest revenue and profit growth engine for IBM during the late 1990s.

The fundamental process or cycle of change is just that simple. This is the 20% that captures 80% of the picture of strategic change:

- **Stage 1:** Do the right thing and do it well.

- **Stage 2:** Discover that the right thing is now the wrong thing.

- **Stage 3:** Do the new right thing, but do it poorly at first.

- **Stage 4:** Eventually do the new right thing well.

Anyone can understand, remember, and recall this framework. If the process is so simple why do a majority of change initiatives fail? The answer lies in the power of the three barriers we mentioned earlier. The failure to see keeps the change process from even getting started. Even when started, the failure to move keeps us from entering the path of the new right thing. Even if we start and move, the failure to finish keeps us from doing the new right thing and doing it well.

With this overall map, we have designed the rest of the book to help you master the challenge of leading strategic change. We dive into the dynamics that drive behavior in each step of our change framework, explore the power of mental maps that can often divert us from successful change, and show how to break through these brain barriers.

In Chapter 2, we examine the first remapping challenge. We investigate why—even when a threat or opportunity is visible—we fail to see it. Clearly, if we fail to see threats or opportunities, we will not make needed changes. In response to this challenge, Chapter 3 details how we can break through this barrier and help others actually see the need to change.

We explore the second barrier to change in Chapter 4. We examine why even when we see, we often fail to move. Although it sounds illogical that we would fail to move if we saw a threat or opportunity, there is ample evidence that failure to move is quite common. Effective change must overcome this powerful mental barrier, and Chapter 5 delivers the keys to overcoming it as we help people actually move once they see the need to change.

The third and final barrier to change consumes Chapter 6. We explore why, even when people move, they often fail to finish—by not moving far or fast enough. Although recognizing the need for change is the thrust that gets us going and moving down the new path lifts us off the ground, if the momentum cannot be maintained, the initial upward lift needed to fly is overpowered by the constant downward pull of gravity. We have seen and studied many cases in which change projects attained initial liftoff, only to falter and crash shortly after clearing the runway. Chapter 7 provides a simple but effective framework for overcoming this challenge and provides the specifics on how to break through this barrier and help people finish a major change initiative.

In Chapter 8, we apply these fundamental principles of change to a central challenge faced by most organizations today. Specifically, we examine how you can lead change in your organization for greater revenue and profit growth.

The next three chapters of *Leading Strategic Change* (Chapters 9, 10, and 11) provide the glue to ensure that all this sticks— sticks together and sticks to you, the reader. This glue is essentially a tool kit for you to lead change in your organization. Not only can this tool kit guide your change leadership, but it can also channel your efforts in training, educating, and empowering others to meet this challenge, as well.

The final chapter (Chapter 12) is perhaps the most important of all. Even though strategic change by its nature takes time to achieve and needs some endurance to produce results, holding on to whatever the strategic change has defined as the new right thing too long will only plunge the company into all the problems that led to the current strategic change in the first place. Consequently, in the final chapter we talk about how to get ahead of the change curve—how to master anticipatory change rather than always being subjected to reactionary or crisis change.

2

Brain Barrier #1: Failure to See

ust imagine that the sun is shining, its rays shimmering off the ocean waves as they lazily break on a smooth, sandy beach. A friendly breeze occasionally rustles the palm trees. You are on the beach because you've done it the old-fashioned way—you've earned it. You've worked hard; you've been smart. You've come up with new technology. You've made your company one of the most recognized in the world. You've pioneered what would turn out to be one of the hottest management concepts of the late twentieth century—6 *Sigma*.[1] You are touted in the press as one of the most admired companies. You are the market leader in what is expected to be one of the largest consumer market products ever—the mobile phone. When it was unveiled, your StarTac phone was the coolest phone to own. You are Motorola.

You are doing the right thing and doing it well. This was the case for Motorola from the late 1980s and into the early 1990s. Its analog phones were the phones to own.

But then the environment shifted—radically. First, a new digital technology for mobile phones came along. However, at first it was not clear how superior the sound would be. In addition, the new digital technology would require new and expensive infrastructure. On top of that, most of Motorola's other U.S. competitors did not seem as though they would make a quick move to the new technology. The one competitor committed to the new technology was some small little company in frozen Finland, a country with a total population of less than that of Manhattan during the day. Besides, no one was really sure how to pro-

---

1. *6 Sigma is a highly disciplined approach to developing and delivering nearly perfect products and services to customers. The core of 6 Sigma focuses on identifying defects in a production process and eliminating them to get as close as possible to zero defects.

nounce the company's name—Nokia. Was it No´-kia (with the emphasis on the "No") or No-kia´ (with the emphasis on the "kia")? And what does a company that has been in the forest products business for over 100 years and excels at making rubber boots for fishermen know about high tech? So what if Nokia went with this new digital phone? So what if countries in Europe adopted this new digital standard? Any of those individual countries, such as Germany or France, paled in comparison to the market size of the United States.

The result? Motorola's first reaction was to deny that this new technology or competitor was anything to worry about.

But then Nokia's revenue increased fourfold, from $2.1 billion in 1993 to $8.7 billion in 1997. All of Europe adopted a common digital standard that allowed people to use their mobile phones virtually anywhere in the region. This convenience drove even greater demand. In the meantime, the fragmented standards of the United States meant that one phone would not necessarily work in every state.

What did Motorola do? Oddly enough, it put even more investment and effort into its analog phones. It did what it knew how to do—what it was good at—and it did it even more intensely than before.

Well, we all know what happened. Motorola's share of global mobile phones dropped from about 35% to just under 15% by end of 2000. Nokia, virtually unknown in the United States in the early 1990s (or most of the rest of the world, for that matter) has become one of the top 5 recognized brands in the world just after GE and before Intel. In 2000, nearly 70% of all mobile phone handset profits went to Nokia, with a market share of around 35%. That's right: Nokia's "profit share" was double its "market share."

BLINDED BY THE LIGHT

Clearly, if you do not see a truck racing toward you, you are unlikely to jump out of the way. Likewise, if you do not realize that you are standing on a treasure of gold, you are unlikely to bend down and pick it up. It is no brilliant observation to say that if people fail to see the need for change (whether threat or opportunity driving it), they will not change.

Everybody knows this. This is why in virtually any book on change there is a section on "creating the need for change." Yes, a felt need for change is required. However, the fact that people fail to see the need or fail to be convinced of the need is compelling evidence that "creating the need for change" is easier said than done. Part of the reason for this is that, by jumping straight to "establish a sense of urgency," we skip over one of the most important questions that provides the necessary insight to help us actually create the need for change.

The question is, Why don't people see the truck or the treasure? Why don't they see the need for change? In almost every case, the need is *not* invisible. If it were invisible, we could hardly blame ourselves or someone else for not seeing the need. But in most cases, the need for change is visible; it is right there in front of us.

For a moment, let's return to the Motorola example. (By the way, we do not mean to pick on Motorola. It has lots of company with other firms that have missed a significant threat or opportunity, such as AT&T, Black & Decker, Caterpillar, IBM, Kmart, Lucent, Merrill Lynch, and Xerox.) Still, although Motorola is not the only firm to miss an important threat or opportunity, the threats and opportunities that Motorola faced were hardly invisible. Yet Motorola still did not see, recognize, or acknowledge them until it was absolutely incontrovertible. Instead, Motorola first denied

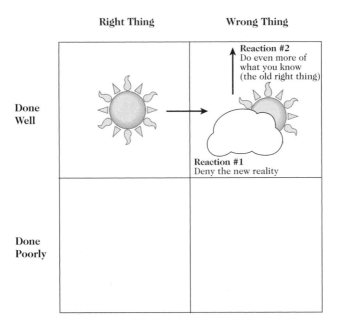

EXHIBIT 2-1
Strategic change matrix: Failure to see.

the threat, then worked harder at what it knew how to do well, as illustrated in Exhibit 2-1

So why do we deny? When we see evidence that a strategy, structure, technology, or product was right in the past but now is wrong, why do we ignore and deny the evidence? To understand the first gravitational force that keeps us from changing, we must come to grips with good answers to these questions.

We deny because we are blinded—blinded by the light of what we already see. To understand what this means, it is important to keep in mind that changes are almost always required in the context of a history, and it is usually a history of success. That history of success creates mental maps in us—maps just as real as those guiding us in the physical world. They tell us where to go and how to get there. For example, consider the map in Exhibit 2-2.

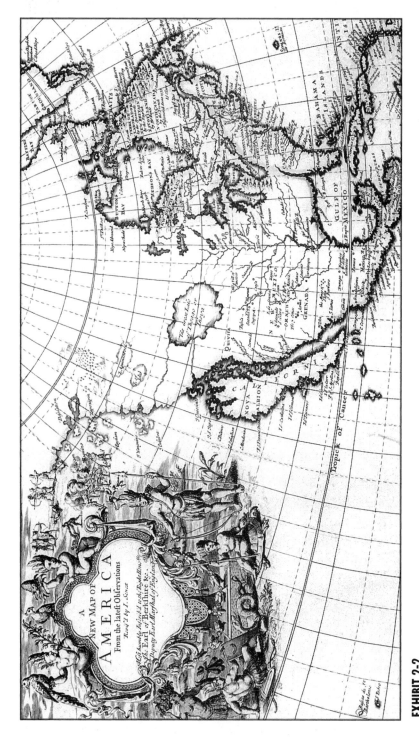

EXHIBIT 2-2
Island of California map.

This is a map of the island of California. When they first see it, many people think it is a futuristic map of California after a huge earthquake—what Californians refer to as the "big one to come." The map is actually quite an old one.

For centuries, Europeans were captivated by legends of distant islands with unimaginable wealth. In 1541, Hernán Cortés and a group of adventurers set sail from Spain to discover such an island. Cortés sailed across the Atlantic, portaged through Mexico, then set sail again up the Strait of California, more commonly known today as the Gulf of Baja. Eventually, his provisions ran low, his crew grew nervous, and he was forced to turn back. To understand this better, it may be helpful to remember that the Gulf of Baja is more nearly 1,000 miles long, or over 1,600 kilometers.

For Cortés, failure was unacceptable, so with a little wishful thinking, he created a success. To the east and west, land was in view; to the north and south, water. Cortés reached a conclusion that seemed perfectly logical: He was in search of an island, and an island he had found—La Isla de California. Cortés returned to Spain and reported to the king and queen exactly what they wanted to hear (and what he wanted to believe): *California is an island.*

Shortly after Cortés's discovery, another expedition was sent to confirm his claim. This one traveled far up along the Pacific coast, past present-day San Francisco. This overly ambitious expedition also ran low on supplies, and by the time they reached the Mendocino River on northern California's coast, the crew was stricken with scurvy. With no inclination to dispute Cortés and no absolute evidence that he was wrong, they concluded that the river was really a strait separating the northern part of the island of California from the rest of the continent.

This cartographic myth persisted throughout Europe for over two centuries. Just imagine if you had this map and landed in what is present-day eastern Texas along the Gulf of Mexico. Your objective was to travel overland and reach the island of California. What would you need to take with you? Boats, of course. You would have to haul boats across what are present-day Texas, New Mexico, and the deserts of Arizona, only to discover that California was not an island. In fact, several expeditions provided clear proof that California was not an island, but it was not until 1745 (200 years after the original map of the island of California was created) that a royal proclamation from Spain finally declared "California is *not* an island."

Why did it take so long for this map to change? Once the belief that California was an island had been established, reports from later explorers were filtered to fit the existing map; anything contradictory was labeled as false or impossible. From all the king knew, the map worked quite well. Why should he throw it away? Similarly, for Motorola, analog phones had worked quite well for a long time. Why should it throw the map away?

Lest we create the impression that only U.S. firms are blinded by the light, let's take a look at one of Nokia's neighbors—IKEA. IKEA is not only one of the largest firms in Sweden, but one of the largest retail furniture companies in the world today.

The mission of IKEA is to create a better everyday life for as many people as possible by making beautiful, functional items for consumers' homes at the lowest possible price. It launched its first catalog in Sweden in 1951. Since then, it has expanded into 22 countries across Europe, North America, Southeast Asia, and Australia. In 2000, it had sales of nearly $9 billion. In sync with its philosophy and mission, its competitive strategy is based on a value proposition of moderate- to good-quality Scandinavian design furniture at incredibly low prices. This strategy works well around the world for most of the products that IKEA offers, such as curtains or dinnerware. However, successful IKEA strategic map failed miserably for some items, specifically beds and sheets, when it expanded into the United States.

When IKEA began its U.S. operations, it shipped low-priced, moderate-quality, *metric*-sized beds and bedding to all of its U.S. stores. It advertised how wonderful the beds were—especially at a full two meters in length! IKEA expected the same great success in the U.S. that it had enjoyed in Europe. Unfortunately, sales did not go well at first. What was IKEA's response? It increased its advertising. Maybe people didn't know what great metric-sized beds IKEA had to offer. More advertising would surely bring customers into the stores and send merchandise flying off the showroom floor.

How did beds and bedding sell in the United States after that? They quickly became category failures, filling up entire warehouses. Local store and regional managers tried to communicate to corporate headquarters in Sweden that metric-sized beds and bedding would not sell in the United States—despite the fact that they were priced lower than the king, queen, full, and twin-sized bedding found in competitors' furniture stores.

How did IKEA's senior managers, who were seven time zones away at corporate headquarters, respond to this local dilemma? "Be more creative. *Pull* the customers into your store. Any good retailer *can* sell metric-sized bedding; that's the solution to your inventory problems." Anders Dahlvig, CEO of IKEA, is quoted as saying, "Whether we are in China, Russia, Manhattan, or London, people buy the same things. We don't adapt to local markets."[2] So, despite local and regional U.S. managers' constant attempts to convince headquarters otherwise, their bosses in Sweden clung to their strategic map for over two years. Finally,

---

2. *Nicholas George, "One Furniture Store Fits All" *Financial Times*, February 8, 2001, p. 11.

the bursting warehouses won, metric-sized beds and bedding were reluctantly discontinued in the U.S. market, and management declared that metric was *not* king; king was king; queen was king; twin was king in the U.S. market.

Why did IKEA persist in following its strategic map of metric as king? Because it had worked so well in the past, and IKEA was good at it. Company leaders could not see an alternative map because their vision was full of the successful and working map they already had.

This is a critical point. If people were blank slates, it would be much easier to put new maps in place when organizations attempt to shift strategic directions. But people are not blank slates. Consequently, one of the first keys to effective change is recognizing that people have existing mental maps, and they have them for only one reason—they have worked and they continue to work well! It is not that "an old dog can't learn *new* tricks." Rather it is that an old dog has a devil of a time unlearning *old* tricks.

Until we recognize that people's vision for the need for change is blocked by existing mental maps that argue for past success and against future change, we will continue to fail in breaking through the first brain barrier of change. We must recognize that people have strong existing mental maps, and we must know what those maps are. Without this understanding, it is almost impossible to overcome people's failure to see.

Successful but Mistaken Maps

As important as this is, it is also critical to understand that, even when using successful maps, people often use mistaken maps. For example, even though the Island of California worked for a while, it was nonetheless inaccurate and full of mistakes. Thus, even when a map has worked well in the past, the seeds of its future failure may lie in that fact that it is inaccurate and mistaken in the first place! This is important because people often believe that if their map works, it must be correct. Consequently, one key to leading strategic change effectively is to recognize and help others see that a map's past success does not necessarily correspond to its correctness.

Interestingly, we have found that these mental mapping mistakes have direct corollaries to common mistakes made with physical maps of the real world. By examining actual maps and their errors, we have gained a much better understanding of the types of mistaken mental maps that people regularly use.

Distorted Maps. Many successful maps have distortions in them that eventually emerge and lead the followers of the map from success to failure. Distorted maps have a tendency to exaggerate some elements of the terrain while diminishing others. This typically reflects the psychological process—found even in cartography—of inflating what you know and deflating what you do not. From a mental map perspective, the extreme state is one in which you believe that what you know is everything and what you do not know is nothing.

How do distorted maps look in actual cartography? Consider the map in Exhibit 2-3.

This is how the United States looks to someone from Boston. As you can see, Cape Cod is of significant size and substance in the Bostonian's mind. On the other hand, although Florida exists, it is quite small in comparison. Likewise, the Northeast in particular and the East in general are much larger than the humble (but no longer an island) California.

Just in case we have any Bostonian readers who are not quite sure what is wrong with this picture, we have also added a map that more accurately portrays the relative dimensions and sizes of the places in question in Exhibit 2-4.

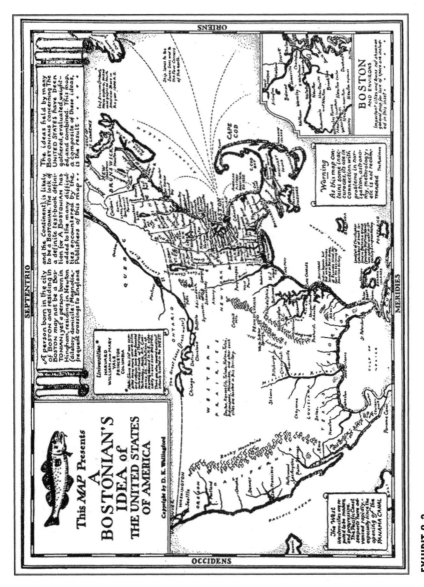

EXHIBIT 2-3

A Bostonian's view of the United States.

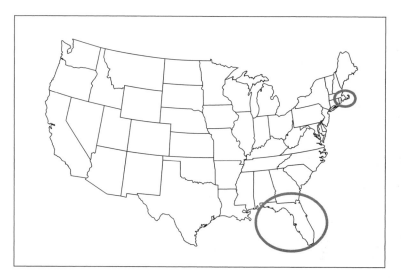

EXHIBIT 2-4
A more accurate view of the United States.

As a point of interest, this type of distortion is common to us all. Asked to draw a map of their neighborhood, people invariably draw their street and house much larger than they are in proportion to the overall neighborhood that they map out.

Although this type of mistaken map is intriguing, the key question is, How does it apply to the business world? The first important implication is that, although a distorted map may be mistaken, it works as long as one does not venture outside of the known area. The distorted map of the United States is not a problem and works well—as long as you stay in New England. Venture off to Florida and use this map to calculate driving time, and the results will not be positive.

The second important implication is that the distorted map leads you to stay within the exaggerated area. Why would you want to leave Boston or New England? After all, based on the map, it looks as though there really is not much else out there. Consequently, using this mistaken map would quite likely cause you to stay "at home." Ironically, staying at home increases the map's success. The more you use it to get around at home, the more successful experiences you will have, and the more convinced you will be that you should hang on to this map. Following the distorted map actually keeps you from encountering evidence of the map's inaccuracies and mistakes!

It is relatively easy to find business examples of these same dynamics that result from relying on a mistaken, distorted map. One of the more interesting examples is the Kellogg's company. Located in Battle Creek, Michigan, Kellogg's has dominated the breakfast table of Americans (especially children) for decades. Kellogg's had a mental map of the world that exaggerated what it knew (breakfast cereal in the United States) and deflated what it did not know (other food products for the rest of the world). As a consequence, Kellogg's view of its existing and new products, as well as existing and new markets, looked like Exhibit 2-5.

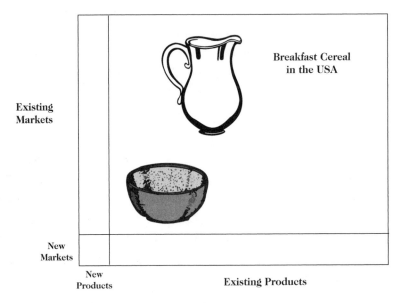

EXHIBIT 2-5
Kellogg's world map of products and markets.

Just as a Bostonian's exaggerated view of the size of Cape Cod, Kellogg's greatly inflated the size of breakfast cereal in the United States, compared with the rest of the picture. For nearly 40 years, this strategic map worked just fine at Kellogg's. As a matter of fact, given how small the rest of the world seemed, based on this map, why should Kellogg's venture far from home, in terms of either products or markets? The prize looked just too small to worry about. So it didn't; it stayed at home within the safe boundaries of its map.

What happens, though, when the home market begins to shift? What happens when people eat breakfast less at the table and more on the run? What happens if generic makers of cereal increase their quality until they begin to rival Kellogg's but offer prices that are 20–30% below Kellogg's? What do you do if you're an executive at Kellogg's? At first, you deny. It is just a temporary blip, and if it is more than temporary, it is confined to a small segment of the market.

What do you do when you see sales start to flag and flatten, and you simply cannot deny the shifts? What do you do when you can deny the shift no longer? You do what you know how to do. You increase trade promotions (i.e., money for retailers to push your product). This is exactly what Kellogg's did, but unfortunately, it did not increase sales much, and it actually hurt the company's earnings.

Based on this distorted mental map of the world, would you explore new products? Look at how small that space is. The answer is that you wouldn't, and Kellogg's didn't. The company did not introduce a single new brand between 1983 and 1991. Even though it successfully introduced Pop-Tarts in 1964, it did not introduce a single new snack-food success until 27 years later, when it launched Nutri-Grain cereal bars.

What about new markets? With this distorted mental map, would you aggressively explore new markets? Again, look at how small that space is. In talking with executives at Kellogg's, several pointed out that they were "into" international markets in a big way during the 1980s and 1990s. The company was operating in roughly 30 different countries. But if you measured revenues and profits and not just countries in which Kellogg's operated, the strategic, financial, and marketing emphases were completely in harmony with the distorted mental map. The vast majority of efforts and returns were focused on the home market. From this case example of Kellogg's, let's review several key points.

First, just because a map works does not mean that it accurately reflects all the terrain. Breakfast cereal in the United States was not nearly as large as it seemed to Kellogg's executives in the context of the global breakfast-food territory.

Second, as long as the terrain in focus doesn't change and you don't venture outside the exaggerated area of focus, the map (mistaken as it may be) continues to work fairly well. The longer it works, the more convinced you become that it is, indeed, correct.

Third, even when signs start to emerge that the map is not working as well today as in the past, its distorted nature creates a logical incentive to stay at home. After all, if the noncereal and non-U.S. parts of the map are as small as they appear, they are not really worth venturing into.

Fourth, even as evidence starts to mount that the terrain has shifted and the map is just plain wrong, there are great pressures to respond to shifts by doing what you know how to do—rather than venturing into unknown territories or paths. Like Kellogg's, you flood the market with sales promotions, rather than make serious attempts to launch new products or conquer new lands.

Until Kellogg's changed its strategic map maker (new CEO, Carlos Gutierrez), no threat or opportunity was seen because Kellogg's was so blinded by the light of what it already saw. Later in the book, we will continue the Kellogg's story and show how it has tried to change the strategic map in executives' heads to grow the company.

Central Position Maps. Another common mistaken map is what we might call *central position maps*. In the world of actual maps, this is the tendency to put yourself (and your country) in the center and have everything else revolve around you.

If you want to do something fun the next time you are in a foreign country, go into a map store and take a look at a world map produced by publishers in that country. Invariably, the map will place that particular country in the center of the world. This tendency has a long history. Perhaps it is best illustrated with an old map of the Central or Middle Kingdom—China. The two Chinese characters that constitute the name *China* literally mean "central or middle kingdom." As the map in Exhibit 2-6 illustrates, China saw herself at the center of the world then, as well as now.

We might think of IKEA as having also viewed the world this way. As its CEO pointed out, "We don't adapt to local markets." It is not the case that IKEA saw Sweden or even Scandinavia as distortedly large and the rest of the world as small. Indeed, it had an accurate map of the size of different furniture markets in the world. Still, IKEA saw itself and its metric measurements as the center of the world. Everything else revolved around it.

As we have already stated, you get a centered map established and accepted only if it works. Metric measures worked for IKEA. For example, IKEA effectively sold metric chairs all around the world, including in the United States. No one in the United States cared (or even knew) that most chairs IKEA sold were .78 meters from the floor to the seat. The more this metric map works, the more you begin to believe that the world revolves around you. With metrics at the center of the universe and with literally billions of dollars of success behind it, why would execu-

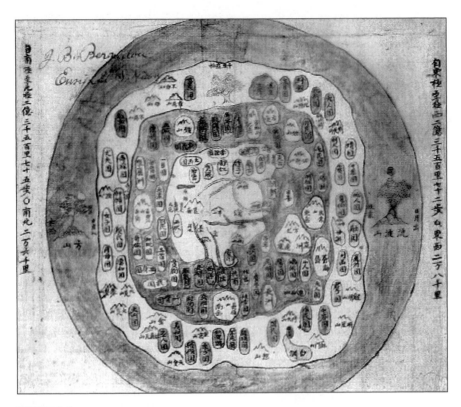

EXHIBIT 2-6
Ancient China as the center of the world.

tives at IKEA *not* resist changing this strategic map? Of course they would resist, and they did.

We need to be careful, however, in providing so many large company examples that we create the impression that only big organizations are subject to these mistakes. These dynamics are just as true for individuals. In the case of central position maps, we also see individuals making this mistake all the time. For example, we knew of a manager sent on an international assignment who had "speak up" at the center of his mental map of interpersonal effectiveness. He explained that "speak up" was the phrase he used (and that the company used) to describe in shorthand the belief that the best way to make decisions, resolve conflicts, and communicate in general was to speak up, to say what you mean and mean what you say. This, he explained, included silence. If you weren't saying anything, it meant that you had nothing to say.

This manager was sent to Thailand. Unfortunately, most of his Thai workers did not share this same mental map of effective interpersonal relations. They were often silent when they, in fact, had things to say. Specifically, they were often silent when they disagreed with this individual. They even said *yes* when they really meant *no*. It did not take this manager long to discover that people said nothing when they had something to say because later their actions did not follow what he thought their silence meant. As these types of experiences began to pile up, he concluded that the Thais did not say what they meant and did not mean what they said.

Using his mental map with "speak up" at the center, he quickly formed interpretations of Thai workers and their behavior. He told us, "These Thais do not say what they mean and I can't trust them to mean what they say. I'm afraid that many of them are just dishonest, weak, and two-faced. With employees like this, I'm not sure we can be successful in this country." He was right. The company had difficulty being successful. However, the firm's struggles were not because of its Thai employees, but rather because of its country manager.

Given his interpretation of the Thai employees, the country manager's course of action was to send some key employees to a training program on speaking up. He pushed what he knew. Interestingly, the more the employees learned about speaking up from the training program, the more they resisted it because they did not think it would work with their Thai subordinates, and they did not want to try and fail.

Speaking up for this country manager in Thailand, like metric for IKEA, was at the center of his map. Things in the past had successfully revolved around this center. The common elements in these situations are that, when the map begins to fail, whether it is for Motorola, IKEA, or an individual manager, the first reaction is to deny the failure, and the second reaction is to try harder by doing even more of what you know how to do best.

Strip Maps. A third type of mistaken map is what we call a *strip map*. A strip map has a restricted or narrow view of the terrain and a fixed sequence for getting from one place to another. Like the other mistaken maps, this one has been with us for a very long time. The strip map in Exhibit 2-7 shows how to get from London to Rome. As you can see, there is a fixed sequence of going from one monastery to the next and a rather narrow view of the path.

Strip maps get established because particular sequences and a narrow path have been shown to work in the past. When we show this old strip map to people, they often laugh. "How could anyone follow such a narrow map?" they ask. When drawn out on paper, strip maps do look rather narrow. How can people fall into the strip-mapping mistake? It is actually quite easy. Although the narrowness of a strip map is obvious when it is drawn out on paper, that narrowness is often missed when the map is seen in our mind's eye. Why? The answer lies in the success of the map. If we follow the strip map sequence, stay within the narrow parameters, and succeed in reaching our desired destination, why would we necessarily think about alternative sequences or other paths off the beaten track to the left or the right? The answer is that we don't. Who has time to argue with success? The sequence worked, so let's not think too much about other alternatives and, instead, simply use the map again.

Consider Barnes & Noble for example. CEO, Lennie Riggio, got his start in selling books when he dropped out of New York Uni-

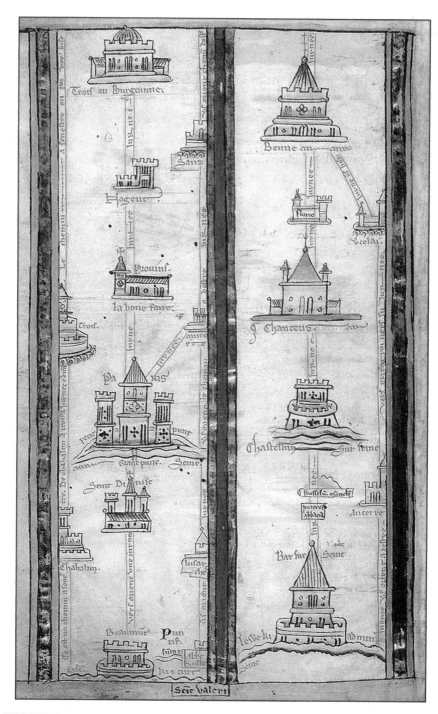

EXHIBIT 2-7
The road from London to Rome.

37

versity in 1965 and opened SBX (Student Book Exchange). By 1971, he owned five SBX college bookstores. That year, he bought a struggling book shop in Manhattan called Barnes & Noble. In 1979, he bought Marboro Books, which had six stores. At this point, the strip map was being established and reinforced. The mental strip map looked something like this: To sell more books, own more brick-and-mortar book shops.

The strip map was further reinforced as more brick-and-mortar bookstores were built. As Riggio built more stores, he also made them bigger. Whereas many of his early bookstores carried 20,000 titles, the newly constructed bookstores carried twice that number. The strip map was further established and reinforced: To get to the destination of more sales, buy or build more brick-and-mortar stores and make them bigger.

The entrenchment of this map solidified when, in 1986, Riggio, using junk bonds and his company, Barnes & Noble (37 total bookstores), bought B. Dalton (over 800 total bookstores). The combination gave Barnes & Noble nearly 850 bookstores, most of them twice the size of the original Barnes & Noble store in Manhattan. In fact, with the acquisition of B. Dalton came not only many larger bookstores, but a few "mega" bookstores, as well. These mega stores carried over 100,000 titles.

Unlike nearly all of its regular big bookstores, which were in shopping malls, the mega bookstores were so big that they were built as separate, stand-alone businesses. Inside these brick-and-mortar shops, Riggio added couches, coffee bars, music CDs, and free copies of the *New York Times Book Review*. Barnes & Noble built scores and scores of these mega bookstores throughout the 1990s. In fact, Barnes & Noble built 95 mega stores in 1995 alone.

By 1995, the strip map was firmly entrenched and reinforced by millions of dollars of success: To sell more books, you need to have (build or buy) *more* and *bigger* brick-and-mortar bookstores. In fact, the map was so successful that even though the U.S. book market grew by less than 1% per year during the

1990s, Barnes & Noble's market share increased from 7% to over 15% during the same time period. This increased share came largely from small, independent bookstores. By July 1998, Barnes & Noble's stock price hit an all-time high of $48, which represented a 220% increase over its price just two years earlier. Barnes & Noble's strip map (Exhibit 2-8) looked brilliant.

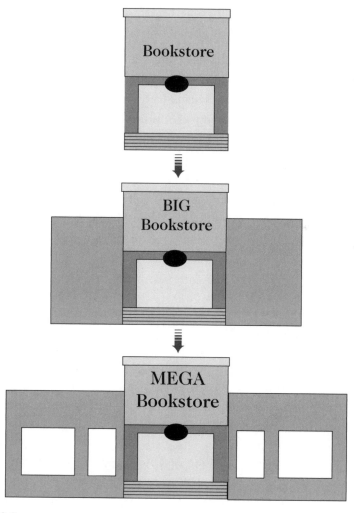

EXHIBIT 2-8
Barnes & Noble's strip map of market success.

What happened? In July 1995, Jeff Bezos, CEO of Amazon.com, decided to follow a different map to selling books. Rather than restrict customers to only 100,000 titles, he would make over a million titles available to them. And rather than have bricks and mortar, customers could click in their orders. For three years, Barnes & Noble totally dismissed Amazon.com. However, when after three years' time, Amazon.com had 8.4 million registered customers and Barnes & Noble had just 1.7 million, shareholders of Barnes & Noble took notice. Many sold their Barnes & Noble stock, and the price tumbled by nearly 50%.

But you may be thinking, "Wait a minute. Look at what has happened to Amazon.com. Its stock price has crashed, and dot-coms are now dot-bombs." This is true. However, just as we were irrationally exuberant about the future of Amazon.com, we run the risk of being irrationally pessimistic about the future of online book sales. We should not confuse Amazon.com's big spending to add everything from CDs to garden tools and the resulting losses as evidence that online book sales will disappear along with Amazon.com's stock price. Online book sales continue to grow and cannibalize book sales from other brick-and-mortar sources. If e-books take off, and we then are able both to order and receive books via the Internet, many predict that online book sales will rival brick-and-mortar-based book sales.

But let's not get sidetracked. The main point is that the strip map of obtaining more sales through more and bigger stores was so entrenched in Barnes & Noble that it took a massive loss in market value before the grip of the mental map and its inherent restriction were changed. In fairness, once recognized in 1998, Lennie Riggio did create Barnesandnoble.com. Unfortunately, at that point, he was playing a serious game of catch-up. By that point, Amazon.com had a 75% percent market share of all online book purchases.

In summary, several key insights grow out of our strip map discussion. First, like all mental maps, strip maps get retained only if they work. A certain sequence of steps and narrowness of territory gets incorporated into a strip map only if it works. Second, as long as you don't venture outside the narrow map, a strip map will likely continue to work. Third, only after a new sequence is proven to work or after a different route to the desired destination is shown to be successful is the old sequence challenged. Unfortunately, by that point, a successful strip map (even if mistaken), like all mental maps, is extremely difficult to change and breaking through this brain barrier is as likely as hitting Mach 1 in a Cessna.

Upright Maps. Whether a mental map is correct or mistaken, the longer it works, the harder it is to change. In a sense, all mental maps successful enough to be retained take on a final characteristic that we see in the world of cartography, as well as in business. This is the tendency to believe that the only way to see the map is the way it has been seen. This is important enough to bear repeating: We mistakenly think that *the only way to see a map is the way it has been seen.* For example, consider the map in Exhibit 2-9. When they first see this map, most people instantly think that it is upside down. After all, Australia is not "up over," it is "down under."

But consider for a moment that you were an alien traveling from a far-off galaxy and you stop your spacecraft by the moon to look at our world. Would north necessarily be up? In zero gravity, isn't it just as reasonable for Australia to be up over as down under? The logical answer is of course, yes. However, when we show this map to people around the world, we invariably find them tilting their heads to one side until the world starts to look right side up again—with the exception of Australians, who think it looks quite right just the way it is.

It is important to note here that, unlike the previous three examples, the traditional right-side-up map is not mistaken and is, in fact, accurate and correct. However, its accuracy and correct-

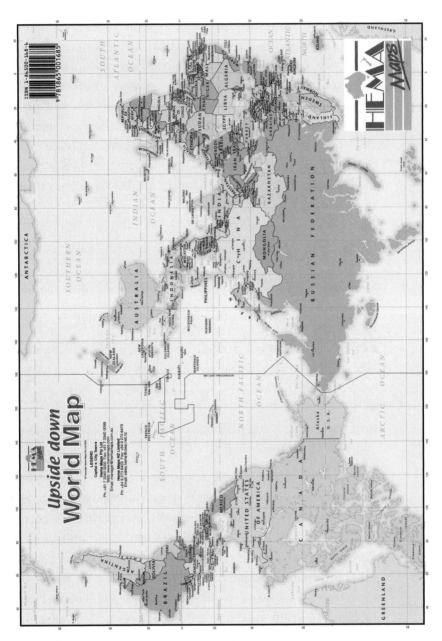

EXHIBIT 2-9

An Australian view of the world. (Map courtesy of www.hemamaps.com.au)

ness are no guarantee that it will continue to work as the only way to get things done. We will come back to this at the end of the book, when we talk about practical things you can do to reduce the chances that you get stuck in holding on to maps that need to change.

Still, the important thing to keep in mind is that, if we see a map a certain way often enough, we end up believing that it is the *only* way for it to be seen. The longer we see the world as consisting mostly of breakfast cereal in the United States, the easier it is to believe that is the only way to see the world. The longer we see metric-measured beds as the center of the world, the easier it is to see metric beds as the only beds. The longer we see bigger brick-and-mortar bookstores as the path to greater sales, the easier it is to see them as the only path. Given enough time and exposure to any map, it becomes the "right" map. As a result, we diminish our capacity to see the world any other way.

OVERCOMING THE FIRST BRAIN BARRIER

Our main points in this chapter are straightforward. First, to fly, we have to understand the power of gravity. The first gravitational force relative to change is that which keeps people from seeing impending threats and opportunities. We have tried to illustrate that people do not see even obvious threats and opportunities because they are blinded by the light of what they already see—the mental maps that have worked for them in the past. Second, we pointed out that even when people have constructed successful mental maps, those maps are quite often flawed. Just as in actual cartography, people create successful but distorted maps, centrally positioned maps, or strip maps. The longer these mistaken maps work (or the longer we believe they work), the more difficult they are to change. Unless we understand the general nature of these mental mapping mistakes, it can be difficult to overcome them. Unless we overcome the power of mental maps, we have little hope of generating enough lift to get our change project off the ground.

3

THE KEYS TO SEEING: CONTRAST AND CONFRONTATION

If people are blinded, how can you help them see? How can you help people see what they have a hard time seeing? How can you avoid getting yourself trapped in past mental maps? You can't just say, "See!" If people could see the shifts and needed changes, they would. The solution has two parts—contrast and confrontation.

Both come from simple facts that we know about actual vision. To see physical objects, we need some contrast in shape, light, and color. We also see best when those objects are directly in front of us, rather than off to the side in our peripheral vision. Even though, in the context of individual and organizational change, we are not talking about seeing physical objects, the two factors that help us see physical objects apply to seeing new business realities just as well.

CONTRAST

As we mentioned, contrast is one of the key means by which the human eye distinguishes different objects. When combined, differences in shape, brightness, and color give us contrast. The letters on this page stand out because of the contrast of black against white. It is such a simple notion that we generally take it for granted. But notice how the contrast lessens as you look at the circles in Exhibit 3-1 from left to right.

EXHIBIT 3-1
Circles of contrast.

In this simple example, the different levels of contrast are easy to see. In complex organizational settings, there are so many things to look at that people can selectively focus on elements from the past and present that are similar, rather than different. In effect, they can choose to ignore key contrasts and thereby avoid looking at why what worked in the past might not work in the future. This brings us to the second part of the answer to overcoming the failure to see—confrontation.

CONFRONTATION

Precisely because the organizational and business realities we face are complex, people can ignore or literally be blind to the "obvious" differences between the past and present. This is why they fail to see the reasons that strategies, structures, cultural values, processes, technologies, etc. must change. The fact that most people do not easily see these contrasts is clear and compelling evidence that people cannot be left on their own to visualize them. Just as we "forced" you to see the contrasts among the circles on the previous page, leaders have to *confront* their people with the key contrasts between the past, present, and future.

COMBINING CONTRAST AND CONFRONTATION

The matrix in Exhibit 3-2 helps to illustrate why both contrast and confrontation are necessary to overcome the first gravitational force—the failure to see.

If there is low contrast (for example, the nearly white circle on the white page) and low confrontation (for example, if you could just skip the previous page on which we presented the contrasting circles), your change efforts are likely to end up in the gar-

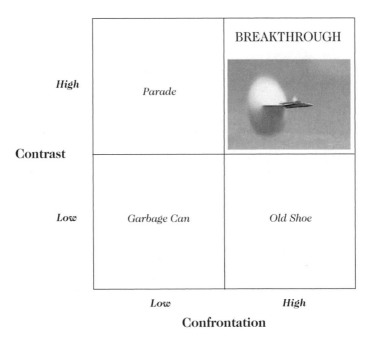

EXHIBIT 3-2
Breaking through the sight barrier.

bage can—wasting time, money, and energy. With low contrast and confrontation, people will not see a need for change and, consequently, won't change.

If contrast is high, however, and confrontation is low, it is like a passing parade. People will "ooh" and "ah" at the difference, but when the parade passes, they will go back to what they were doing before.

If confrontation is high but contrast is low, it is like an old shoe. It sits there confronting you every day, but it is still the same old shoe. It looks and smells no different each day.

The key to overcoming the failure to see is creating both high contrast *and* high confrontation. Unfortunately, this is much easier said than done. Even when leaders attempt to create both high contrast and confrontation, we frequently observe two common mistakes.

Mistake #1: The Comprehensiveness Mistake. In creating high contrast, one of the first mistakes many leaders make is what we call the *comprehensiveness mistake*. The mistake happens as leaders try to illustrate the contrasts between yesterday and tomorrow but end up making the illustration too complex and comprehensive. When presented with a complex picture of the past and present (or future), the complexity actually allows employees to focus on what they want. Because people are programmed to hang on to what has worked, they are likely to use that freedom to focus on similarities in the picture, rather than differences. Why? Similarities reinforce past mental maps, whereas differences may threaten them. Presenting too complex a picture also allows people to zero in on the "not so important" contrasts, rather than the critical one. Either way, people are free to conclude, "Things are not really that different." And if things are not really that different, then little need exists for them to think or behave differently. The important thing to keep in mind is that the more complex the picture presented is, the more alternative specific points there will be on which people can choose to focus. This, in turn, increases the chances that they will select the wrong targets for guiding their actions.

What causes leaders to make this common mistake? In some cases, the cause of this comprehensiveness mistake is that leaders know that reality is complex, and they do not want to appear to be simple-minded. Consequently, they list and discuss "a variety of factors contributing to our need to change." At one level, this is quite understandable and sensible. Yet in our experience, the true cause of this mistake is less admirable. In most cases, the mistake has *less* to do with a desire to "reflect the complex reality of the current business environment" and *more* to do with leaders' inability or unwillingness to identify the core of the issue. Rather than take the time and energy to identify the core 20% that accounts for 80% of the problems, they fall for an easier approach of simply listing all the factors. The time and brainpower required to create a long list of factors is not nearly that required to determine which factors on that long list are the most influential. This is why calling this the *comprehensiveness mistake* is too polite; we probably ought to call it the *laundry list mistake*.

Mistake #2: The "I Get It" Mistake. Even if we as leaders are successful at avoiding the first mistake (the comprehensiveness mistake), there is a second pitfall we all too often see people fall into—the "I get it" mistake. The mistake is simple. It is presenting the contrast once and only once. In other words, as the leader, you recognize the need for change, so you present it to others one time and expect them to understand it instantly. After all, you understand it, so why shouldn't they?

When we say "you," we mean everybody. No one seems to be totally immune from making this mistake. So why do we make this mistake? The answer lies in giving ourselves too much credit. After we spend time trying to understand a problem and the light bulb in our head finally turns on, we give ourselves too much credit and forget how much time and effort it took to "get it." This happens in part because once we get it, we get it. The neural pathways in our brain among the various components of the problem and solution are established. They are there. Once we understand it, we do not have to do anything to understand it again. The neural pathways are paved, and we can make the connections at high speeds. It is there; we see it instantaneously. In fact, we often think, "This was so obvious. Why didn't I see it from the start?" It is as though once the light goes on, it turns off our memory of how we got there and how much time and effort it took.

Consequently, we think that if we mention it once to someone, they will get it, too. The new strategic vision is so obvious, how many times should we need to repeat it? During consulting engagements, we have heard leaders on many occasions ask us something similar to the following: "Didn't they hear me? I explained all this in my presentation the other day. Are they brain dead?" Although this may seem harsh, we can't even print the harsher statements. But the key point is that all of us give ourselves too much credit and forget how many times we had to look at a problem, how many different angles we had to explore, and how long we had to think about it before we finally understood it. Because we forget the process of understanding it, we end up thinking that saying it once to others is more than enough for them.

CREATING HIGH CONTRAST

With these two common mistakes in mind, we can now turn our attention to specific means of creating high and compelling contrast—the first of our two-part solution. Given the tendency to try to paint pictures that are too complicated and comprehensive, effective contrast requires leaders to focus on the core 20%. As we have already pointed out, reality in its entirety is complex. Left completely in its complexity, the important contrasts are hard to see. Consequently, leaders have to simplify and focus on the key differences. The key is identifying the *key* differences. Making the judgments as to what are and what are not core contrasts is what leaders get paid for.

Imagine for a moment that you work for the leading signal processing firm, QuadQ, Inc.,[1] whose products primarily ship to the health care industry. Scientific researchers and hospital researchers use your products in diagnostic tests and cellular and blood chemical analysis. QuadQ's analog technology has been at the leading edge for years. Then a shift occurs in the

---

1. *QuadQ, Inc. is a fictitious name but represents a real but disguised situation.

market. First, digital signal processing emerges as a competing technological platform. When it first emerges, however, it seems unable to rival your analog technology. Second, the nature of customers begins to shift. Diagnostics and analyses are done increasingly in clinics and by technicians, not in research labs by MDs and PhDs. Third, there is a trend to coordinate separate tests and analyses into integrated systems. The emerging "buzz phrase" in your industry becomes "providing solutions, not boxes, to customers."

As signs of these shifts first emerge, many of the scientists within your firm resist the signals that the environment is changing. They work harder at coming up with customized analog solutions for customers. Over a year or two, it becomes increasingly clear to you that digital signal processing is the superior technology in general and specifically for integrating your products into larger solutions. It also becomes more evident to you that digital is the way to go for simplifying the use of your product so that less sophisticated customers can operate the equipment.

How do you create a compelling contrast sufficient to shake your employees free from their entrenched mental maps? First, you have to cut to the core. What are the core contrasts between the past and the future? Clearly, QuadQ exists in a very complex environment, but allowing too much of that complexity to creep in can kill the needed contrast.

Although QuadQ's environment is full of complexity, five key contrasts exist: technology, strategy, customers, competencies, and relationships (Exhibit 3-3). Keep in mind that, as simple as this seems, it still requires people to remember 10 things (i.e., five categories by two descriptions). This is important when you recall, as we previously mentioned, that although most people can remember seven things, only about 2% remember ten. You create the following matrix to highlight the core contrast.

EXHIBIT 3-3   QuadQ's Changing Environment

ISSUE	OLD	NEW
Technology	Analog	Digital
Strategy	Make leading-edge boxes	Provide leading-edge solutions
Customers	Hospital and research centers. Sophisticated doctors and scientists	Clinics and labs. Significantly less sophisticated technicians
Key Personal Competencies	Scientific and technical brilliance	Teamwork
Departmental Relations	Autonomous and independent	Collaborative and cooperative

The second thing you do is ratchet up contrast by enhancing the conceptual distance between the descriptions. You know that the reality may not be quite so black and white, but you also know that the greater the contrast, the easier it is for employees to see difference and recognize the acute need for change.

In addition to focusing on the core contrasts, you also take a page from what we know in general about vision and memory. Research has clearly demonstrated that the better you create images in people's minds, the more clearly they can recall associated messages. Although the above matrix appeals to your cerebral nature, you realize the need for something else—something more visual. In response, you create a very simple picture that contrasts the old and the new, as shown in Exhibit 3-4.

Using these images, you explain that in the past, individual, brilliant scientists created leading-edge analog boxes that very sophisticated customers used. That was the old map. The new map calls for gearing products toward increasingly less sophisticated customers and away from doctors and research scientists. With the new map, QuadQ will create more integrated, digital

Old Map

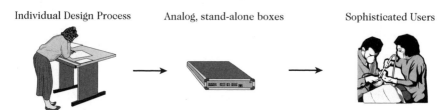

Individual Design Process   Analog, stand-alone boxes   Sophisticated Users

New Map

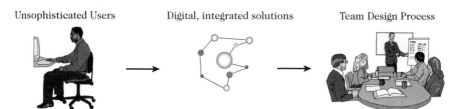

Unsophisticated Users   Digital, integrated solutions   Team Design Process

EXHIBIT 3-4
QuadQ's strategic contrast maps.

solutions, rather than boxes. Finally, instead of relying on individual brilliance among QuadQ scientists, the future will require cross-functional teams composed of technology, marketing, and manufacturing people to design and produce the new solutions.

To summarize, you have three steps for creating high contrast:

1. Focus on the core 20% of what is different.
2. Enhance (even slightly exaggerate) the simple descriptions between the old and new.
3. Create visual images, or pictures, of the old and new so that the contrast is understood as more than mere words.

CREATING CONFRONTATION

Clearly, pointing out contrasts between the old and new is a critical first step to change. However, to avoid the "I get it" mistake, pointing these contrasts out just once is not enough. Twice is not enough. To ensure a high level of confrontation, you will likely have to present the contrasts repeatedly so employees don't view them as "one-time passing parades" that they can simply wait out. For example, remember the Australian map of the world from Chapter 2? Let's look at it one more time.

When viewing the map this time (if you're *not* Australian), did a small voice inside your head still say, "That's upside down"? If so, consider yourself quite normal. Now imagine how much exposure to this map it would take to get rid of that voice in your head—to *completely* eliminate it. That's why repetition becomes so important when trying to change mental maps. But just how many repetitions are enough as you try to initiate change at work? Unfortunately, we know of no scientific studies that answer this question. From our observations and conversations with seasoned executives, though, employees need to hear the contrast message clearly at least five or six times to ensure that they get it.

Repetition is a powerful, but certainly not the only, means of ensuring high confrontation. An additional means is employing what we call *inescapable experiences*. An inescapable experience has two dimensions. The first is (get ready for this) that it is inescapable. By this we mean that it is hard for the individual to mentally sidestep or ignore the experience or to physically walk away from the experience. Second, the experience must be (again get ready for this revelation) experiential. This may sound redundant, but the experience cannot be just mental. It needs to actively involve as many of the senses as possible: touch, smell, sight, sound, taste. We know from a wide body of scientific literature that the more senses involved and the deeper their involvement, the higher will be the impact of an experience—more is learned, and more is retained.

Let's return to QuadQ, Inc. As the CEO, you did a good job of creating contrast, but you must also ensure effective confrontation. The message must be repeated—probably more often than you think necessary. In addition, you must create some inescapable experiences. How can you do this? You might borrow a page from the CEO of Samsung Electronics.

Samsung is a giant conglomerate in Korea, and Samsung Electronics is one of its key companies. Samsung Electronics is, by most accounts, the leading consumer electronics company in Korea. It has the largest market share and a premiere quality image. It was used to operating in a certain way. Yet its operations and sales in the United States were not going well at all. The CEO was convinced that Samsung had to operate differently in that market than at home, but the message was just not getting through to his top managers in Korea. So the CEO created an inescapable experience. He put nearly 100 of the most senior executives on a plane, and off they went to visit stores in the United States.

The contrasts were stark. Rather than being sold in small shops as in Korea, electronics were sold in large stores in the United States. Rather than getting prime merchandising space as they did in Korea, Samsung products were in the bargain bin, back behind leaders such as Sony, and even behind second-tier makers, such as GE. Samsung executives saw where their products were displayed, rubbed their fingers across the dust on the products, heard customers talk excitedly about competitors' product features as they shopped, and tasted the envy in their mouths for the position of market leaders such as Sony. Samsung was king at home but not in the royal court in the United States.

Samsung executives could not escape the experience. It was repeated essentially a dozen times as the group went from store to store. They could not sidestep the experience because they were physically put in the center of it. As a consequence, the contrast finally had a deep impact.

As the CEO of QuadQ, you should do something similar. You must create an inescapable experience. Simply talking about the contrasts, even repeatedly, is not enough. What can you do? Let's take a look at the Samsung example for insights.

First, the primary objective of an inescapable experience is putting people directly in front of the most important and forceful aspects of the contrast. As a consequence, you must decide what you want the experience to focus on. Just as there is the danger of diluting the impact of contrast by allowing too much complexity, so too can you dilute the impact of the confronting experience by making it too complex and unfocused. In the case of Samsung, what was a core contrast that hit the executives right between the eyes? It was the treatment of the product. To exaggerate, in Korea, Samsung's products are held respectfully in gloved hands when presented to consumers. In the United States, they're casually tossed into bargain bins with a sign above reading "Clearance Sale!"

What is the key contrast that can hit QuadQ employees, especially the scientists, right between the eyes? Customers. QuadQ scientists are used to interacting with other PhD scientists wearing lab coats. QuadQ scientists are used to creating sophisticated solutions for other lab coat-type customers. What would happen, though, if you confronted your PhD scientists with a new technician-type customer holding only an associate's degree, sporting purple hair, and wearing a nose ring? Then what would happen if you sat that less formally educated customer down to run diagnostics on your old analog products, and your PhD research scientists were forced to listen to the customer's severe complaints about the products? The contrast—if done with enough new-generation customers over a long enough period of time—would be compelling and inescapable. The resulting shock is precisely what your people need for you to have a prayer of overcoming the strength of their old analog map that has dominated the strategic path of success in your firm for the last 40 years.

To summarize, two steps create high-impact confrontation.

1. Repeat the messages of the old and new maps *over* and *over* and *over* again.

2. Create high-impact, inescapable confrontations.

   a) Focus the experience on what you think are the core contrasts. Do not dilute it with too much complexity.

   b) Make sure that the experience involves as many of the senses as possible. There are few effective substitutes for live, fully engaged action.

   c) Physically ensure that people cannot easily avoid the experience but must take the brunt of it right between the eyes.

PULLING IT ALL TOGETHER

Contrast and confrontation—these two keys break through the first brain barrier and conquer the failure to see. Although we may not have said it explicitly, you no doubt have sensed that changing entrenched mental maps requires a serious shock to the system. In closing, let us make that point clear and unmistakable. The longer a given mental map has been in place and the more successful it has been, the greater will be the shock needed to break free from it.

As evidence of this, consider some personal, managerial maps, rather than organizational maps. Most managers grow up in a given country and culture, be that Germany, Australia, Japan, or India. They develop managerial maps of how to communicate, motivate, correct, praise, confront, and direct people successfully. This generally works fine until, as a senior leader in most companies today, you must interact effectively with people across multiple countries and cultures—i.e., global leadership. Recently, we conducted a study along with a colleague, Allen

Morrison, looking at what experiences helped people develop global leadership capabilities. When we asked over 130 senior executives from 55 different companies across Europe, North America, and Asia what the most important and influential experience was in helping them develop global leadership capabilities, 80% gave the exact same answer. Given the diversity of these executives (different nationalities, job histories, industries, etc.), this is amazingly high agreement. Eight of ten executives said an international assignment was the most influential career experience they had. Why?

The following example provides the answer. Not long ago, we, along with our colleague Allen Morrison, were on a trip to Japan for an international management conference. Because one of our trio, Stewart Black, had lived and worked in Japan before, he decided to take the other two to a traditional Japanese restaurant for dinner. Being the interculturally sensitive guy that he is, he gave the other two a "briefing" about the restaurant and proper etiquette before going in. He explained that most traditional Japanese restaurants have a similar entry. It consists of a thin wood and glass sliding door with an entry area on the other side. The runners at the bottom of the door, along which it slides, are made of wood and typically not recessed; consequently, he warned the other two that they would need to step carefully over them as they entered the restaurant. He then mentioned that they would be in a small alcove called a *genkan* and that they would remove their shoes before stepping up into the restaurant proper.

Once they found what looked like a nice, traditional restaurant, Stewart opened the sliding door and carefully stepped inside. Allen, who is about the same height as Stewart, followed, also being sure to step over the door runner. The next thing anyone knew, there was a thunderous crash at the entry that reverberated throughout the entire restaurant. Everyone inside turned to see what had happened; some customers thought an earthquake had started. As everyone looked to the restaurant entry, they saw Hal staggering in the doorway with a trickle of blood running down his forehead. Hal, on seeing his two colleagues negotiate the entry so easily, had tried to step quickly through the door. However, Hal, who is just over 6'5", smashed his head on the top of the door frame. The impact nearly knocked Hal out.

The most interesting part of this story is that the next day, when the trio went to another traditional Japanese restaurant, the exact same thing happened. Now Hal had twin bumps on his head. It wasn't until the third time that Hal remembered to duck as he entered. It took getting smacked hard in the head—twice—for Hal to rearrange his mental map about what it takes for him to enter a traditional Japanese restaurant successfully.

Most of us are like Hal. It takes getting smacked hard in the head, probably more than once, before we are ready to rearrange what is in our heads—our mental maps. Hard knocks to the head are not always pleasant—in fact, they hurt—but they are necessary.

International assignments, unlike short trips, almost always result in some serious smacks to the head. We are confronted on a daily basis with managerial situations in which our old maps do not work. Because we cannot easily hide out in our hotel rooms for three years, we eventually smack our heads—hard and usually repeatedly. This head smacking is what caused the global leaders we interviewed to change their managerial mental maps. And this is why eight of ten touted an international assignment as the most important developmental experience in their careers and their development as global leaders.

The point is not that everyone should go on an international assignment (though if you want to be a global leader, you may need to). Rather, the point is to illustrate that a smack in the head with contrast and confrontation is often needed to dislodge entrenched mental maps. These smacks are what help us see that our mental maps have limits and to deal with shifts in the environment; we must stretch and rearrange our maps—as painful as that might be.

Brain Barrier #2: Failure to Move

In the previous chapter, we voted you in as CEO of QuadQ, Inc., the signal processing firm. We now want to return you to that role. Recall that your products primarily go to the health care industry, and in the past, they were used by scientific and hospital researchers in diagnostic tests, as well as cellular and blood chemical analysis. Your analog technology has defined the leading edge for years. However, the leading-edge technology has shifted from analog to digital, the market from sophisticated customers to technicians, and products from stand-alone boxes to integrated solutions.

Finally, after two separate task forces are formed and independently craft the conclusions mentioned above, most technical and scientific personnel in your firm capitulate. They throw their arms up and exclaim, "Digital signal processors *are* the future." Their old mental maps of how the world works are broken. Your matrix, your pictures, and even your customer experience all produced their intended effect. You even polished your vision speech:

Folks, we are facing a brave new world. Technology is shifting from analog to digital signal processing. Our strategy and competitive advantage have always been and will remain our leading-edge technology. We must embrace this new technology. In addition, our customers are shifting from hospitals, sophisticated doctors, and research scientists to clinics and technicians. With this shift in customers, our products must become more "user friendly" and simpler to operate. Furthermore, we cannot afford simply to make boxes. We must provide more integrated solutions. To accomplish this, we must work more in teams. We need R&D, engineering, marketing, and sales to work in cross-functional teams so that we fully incorporate changing customer needs into the design of our products from the start. In addition, speed to market will be critical to our future success, which will require greater coordination and cooperation across various departments. *Simpler, speedier solutions!* This is the vision!

You hired a consultant. (Oops, that may be a mistake. Hope you hired the right one.) You followed this book's advice (good move), and you communicated, communicated, and communicated the vision—the new map. You sent out e-mails; you made a couple of short videos for broadcast during lunches in the company dining room; you made several PowerPoint presentations to different groups and departments. You kept your message consistent and concise.

Now you sit back and wait to see what you view as the inevitable change within your company. You wait and you wait and you wait. Nothing changes; no one moves. What's going on?

You're perplexed. If they see that the old right thing is now wrong and that digital signal processing is the future, why aren't they moving in that direction? You just don't get it. After all, you read the first few chapters of this book and followed our advice. You broke through the first brain barrier. People see that the old right things are now wrong. Why aren't they moving?

People now not only see that the old right thing is wrong, but they also have a clear idea of what the new right thing is, right? You have made the vision clear. Oddly, you begin to feel as though the clearer you make the vision and the more you repeat it, the more resistance to movement you begin to feel.

This illustrates the continued gravitational force against change and the second brain barrier—*failure to move.* For most people we talk with, the first brain barrier makes more intuitive sense than the second. Most people understand quite easily that if people don't see the need for change, they are unlikely to change. But if people begin to see the need for change, why would they fail to move? After all, not jumping out of the way of a truck heading right for you because you didn't see it is one thing. But failing to move after you see the truck bearing down on you is quite another. Are people who see but still fail to move just plain dumb?

Smart People don't Try New Tricks

In our experience, people who fail to move even after they see the need are *smart*, not dumb. To understand clearly why they fail to move even when they see the need and why this is smart, not dumb, we need to break the second barrier into two parts.

The first part involves the distinction between seeing that the old right thing is now wrong and seeing the new right thing. The first does not necessarily lead to the second. That is, just because someone finally capitulates and admits that the old right thing is wrong does not mean that they see the new right thing. Because of this, people will fail to move if the new right thing is not clear.

Consider Xerox. It has had a history of doing the right thing well. Early in its history, it focused on making copiers for businesses. They were big and expensive, and they made the company tons of money. Unfortunately for Xerox, the environment shifted. The right thing ended up being the wrong thing. For example, Canon came along and introduced the personal copier for a price that was one-tenth the cost of Xerox's low-end machines. At first, Xerox denied the shift in the market until it was almost too late. Xerox viewed personal copiers as a novelty item instead of a serious business line. Early on, the company even refused to leverage a personal copier created by its joint venture in Japan with Fuji (FujiXerox). Finally, Xerox responded and regained a respectable position in the personal copier segment. Yet in the mid-1990s, Xerox once again faced the challenge of strategic change.

To tackle this transformation, Rick Thoman—a key player in IBM's dramatic turnaround—was brought onboard to lead the transformation. When he came to Xerox, he laid out a principal vision that was quite similar to the vision that successfully transformed IBM in the early 1990s—a new strategic map that propelled IBM's stock price from nearly $40 to $200 (split adjusted). IBM's vision demanded solutions (not just boxes) for customers through global ISUs (industry solution units). The fundamental notion at IBM was that customer solutions within a given industry would be more similar than solutions across industries. In other words, a solution for Citigroup would be more similar to a solution for Bank of Tokyo-Mitsubishi than a solution for Exxon-Mobil. IBM determined that firms' needs within a given industry (such as banks) were more similar to each other than they were to firms in other industries.

IBM's strategy and structure were designed not just to make sense, but also to make money. The view was that if IBM could utilize 50–70% of a solution it had created for Citigroup for Bank of Tokyo-Mitsubishi as well, it could extract significant margins. After all, Citigroup would have already paid full price for the solution IBM developed for it. IBM would then charge Bank of Tokyo-Mitsubishi full price, but in one sense, part of the solution for Bank of Tokyo-Mitsubishi would have already paid for. In many ways, the new strategy and structure worked wonderfully, and as we mentioned earlier "services" became a major source of IBM's revenue and profit growth during the mid- to late1990s.

As the new CEO, Thoman delivered a similar vision to Xerox. Customers needed document solutions, not just copiers. Customers grouped by industry would have more similar needs and, therefore, require more similar solutions than customers grouped by geography (territories) as in the past. This constituted the new strategic map for a new Xerox.

However, the mental maps for many Xerox employees were radically different. Xerox sales and service organizations had been organized largely by geographic territory. As a consequence,

Xerox sales people knew customers within their sales territory well, regardless of what industry they were in. Yet, as deteriorating financial results mounted and Xerox stock price dropped into a near free fall, evidence piled up that the old way was just not right anymore. Thus, the old "geographic sales" and "copiers" strategic maps began to crumble, making way for a new "document solutions" map.

Still, people within Xerox failed to change. Why? Why did people fail to move when it became crystal clear that what used to work in the past didn't work at all in the present? As we already mentioned, remember that, even if we see that the old right thing no longer works, we still don't move if the new map with its destination and path is not clear. After all, how reasonable is it to venture out into the dark and unknown just because it feels a bit uncomfortable where you are sitting today? And as strange as it may seem, even if we cannot deny that the old right thing is now wrong, when lacking a new right direction, we often simply intensify our efforts at doing what we do know.

Terrific. But Rick Thoman did deliver his new vision for Xerox. He presented the vision, strategy, and new structure clearly and repeatedly to Xerox employees. Yet in this case (and many others that we have witnessed), people still failed to move. In fact, people so dramatically failed to move at Xerox that Thoman was forced out of the company less than two years after assuming the helm.

To understand in the real case of Xerox and in the fictional case of QuadQ, let's take a minute to recap. First, we pointed out that, even when people see that the old right thing is now wrong, they fail to move if they do not see the new right thing. This makes sense and is one reason why everyone talks about "articulating the new vision." However, in the case of Xerox as well as QuadQ, the new vision was not only articulated but repeated. So why, even when people finally acknowledge the need for change and see the new direction, do people often still fail to move.

Of the two parts, the second is clearly the most perplexing. After all, it is one thing for people to fail to move if they recognize the need but are not given a new direction to march in, but it is quite another for people to fail to move even after the new vision is clearly presented and understood.

But the most perplexing and paradoxical thing we have consistently observed is that quite often the *clearer* the new vision, the *more* immobilized employees become. How can this be? We just argued in the previous two chapters that leaders must create in people a recognized need for change, then show them the new direction. How can it be that often—actually, all too often—the clearer the vision and new strategic map, the more immobilized people become?

Our experience tells us that this happens because people are smart. So how can *not* moving be smart, even when it is clear that the old right thing is now wrong and the new right thing is brilliantly illuminated? It is smart because people recognize that there are two sides to the story. The first side focuses on the "right thing" and the "wrong thing." The second emphasizes "doing it well" and "doing it poorly" (see Exhibit 4-1).

People recognize that they cannot go directly from doing the wrong thing well to doing the new right thing well. They understand that they will go from doing the *wrong* thing *well* to doing the *right* thing *poorly*. Given this brilliant insight, imagine from their perspective how silly a leader shouting for change might seem. Essentially, from their perspective, the leader is saying, "Follow me and you will do the right thing and you will do it *poorly*!" How appealing is that? Yet even if the leader has no intention of communicating this message, people know that is exactly what is going to happen. They are so smart that, even if you don't see it or even if you try to hide it, they are not fooled.

No one expects to be instantly great at something they have not done before. This is part of the reason that we don't take up new

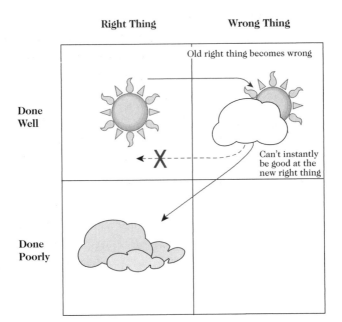

EXHIBIT 4-1
Strategic change matrix: Breaking through the movement barrier.

languages, sports, musical instruments, and so on with greater frequency. Most of us do not like to be bad at something, especially if we are already good at something else.

That is why, for most people, going from being competent to incompetent is a very unappealing proposition. Ironically, this is also why the clearer the vision of the new right thing, the more immobilized people often become. The clearer the new vision, the easier it is for people to see all the specific ways in which they will be incompetent and look stupid—ways that they will do the right thing and do it horribly.

For example, let's once again return to the case in which you are the CEO of our signal processing company, QuadQ, Inc. At first, the company's performance began to deteriorate because people were trapped in old mental maps of success. As evidence mounted and you provided the needed contrast and confrontation, employees began to see that the old right thing was not right any more. Even with this recognition, though, they failed to move at first because they could not see what new direction to move in—the future vision was not clear. This makes sense. No one wants to take a walk in the dark. Then you clearly illuminated the future vision and map. Yet the more clarity you added, the easier it was for people to see and anticipate (because they are smart) what they were going to soon be terrible at.

Consider the scientists and engineers in the firm who had made their careers in analog technology. As the digital future became clearer, so did their visions of their future incompetence. As readers with backgrounds or exposure to these two disciplines know, moving from analog to digital as a scientist or engineer is not an overnight process. In many ways, it is like having learned Chinese, then being told to pick up Greek over a long weekend. Yes, both are languages, and having learned one, you may have developed some general language-learning capabilities, but learning Greek from a Chinese base is almost like starting over. In fact, the clearer the differences between the Chinese you know and the Greek that you do not, the easier it is for you to anticipate how difficult it will be to learn Greek and how bad you will be at speaking it. You can easily imagine how many mistakes of grammar, pronunciation, usage, and so on you will make. You can see a movie in your mind's eye about how stupid you will look. The clearer the images of how dumb you will look making these mistakes, the less you want to move toward learning Greek. Back at QuadQ, the more the scientists and engineers saw that digital signal processors were the future, the more they saw how bad they were going to be and how incompetent they were going to look.

The same dynamic applies to many other aspects of the new vision. Your scientists and engineers had made their careers through technical brilliance as star individuals. In fact, knowledge or understanding of "inferior" areas in the past, such as marketing, was definitely a negative—not a positive. (By the way, your QuadQ scientists didn't even dignify areas such as marketing or sales by calling them *disciplines*; they were *functions*, not *disciplines*.) If working in cross-functional teams was required for success in the future, some cross-functional understanding would also be required. What did these scientists know about working in cross-functional teams? What did they even know about working on technical teams that tried to deliver integrated solutions? Nothing. How good at teams in general, and in cross-functional teams in particular, were they going to be? Terrible. The scientists and engineers could see this. The clearer you made the vision, the more you repeated it, the easier it was for your scientists to see how bad they would be. What did they do? They resisted. Why? Because after a life devoted to being brilliant, they did not want to look stupid.

The same dynamic was true at Xerox. The clearer the vision about solutions and ISUs, the easier it was for sales people to see how bad they were going to be. After all, what did they know about delivering solutions? Nothing. What did they know about working in industry-focused teams? Nothing. Consequently, how good at it were they likely to be? Terrible. Because they were smart, not dumb, they did not want to look or feel stupid. Add to this mix a culture in which mistakes were often punished and learning was rarely rewarded, and you must wonder who would want to venture off into the land of certain incompetence and probable punishment when they could stay in the home country of demonstrated capabilities and peer respect? No one.

Some might argue that the vision, strategy, and structure that Thoman brought to Xerox were wrong for the company, that Thoman inappropriately just took what he knew and what had worked at IBM and forced it on Xerox. Perhaps. It is hard to know for sure. Many thought the vision, strategy, and structure that Gerstner (with Thoman's help) implemented at IBM were wrong until they began to work. Perhaps those who thought the vision, strategy, and structure that Thoman brought to Xerox were wrong would be singing a different tune if they had delivered results. Our main point is that the vision might have worked, had Xerox employees actually seen a path from doing the right thing poorly to doing it well. In other words, many preferred to be *competent at the wrong thing* than *incompetent at the right thing.* As long as they saw a future filled with doing the right thing poorly, most employees were not inclined to move. Our point is that movement was unlikely until employees plainly saw a promising path to the promised land.

Although the details of creating a "promising path" is a key focus of Chapter 5, the point we want to stress here is that people fail to move even when they see the need because most will do just about anything to avoid doing the new right thing and doing it poorly. Not only do people need to see the new direction or destination, they must see and—more importantly—*believe* in a path to take them from doing the right thing poorly to doing it well. Without this prospect, many people prefer competence at the wrong thing to incompetence at the right one.

As mentioned earlier, most change books and change consultants harp on the need to provide a vision of the future—a new direction or destination. We agree. Most of us are not too keen on venturing out into the dark, especially if there is a safe light still on where we are. On this point, we are reminded of the old joke about a man who lost his ring. He searches madly for it, and along comes a stranger asking, "What did you lose?" "My ring," he replies. "Where did you lose it?" asks the passerby. "Way over there," the man frantically answers. "Then why are you looking here?" queries the intended helper. "Because this is where the light is," replies the hopeless searcher. In organizations, people also stay where the light is, even when they recognize that it is the wrong place. People often stick to what they are good at, even when they see that it has become irrelevant.

OVERCOMING THE SECOND
BRAIN BARRIER

To summarize, two keys make it possible to overcome gravity and break through the second brain barrier to change. First, even after we have helped people see that the old right thing is now wrong and we have painted a picture of the new right thing, that new map must have a clear destination or vision. The map must answer the question, Where are we going? Yet this is not enough. In fact, the clearer the answer to where we are going, in many cases the greater will be the resistance to getting there because people can now see how bad they will be at doing the new right thing. Consequently, along with illuminating the new right thing, we must create a belief in people that new Strategic map includes a promising path that will guide them through doing the right thing poorly to doing it very well.

It is this part of the second brain barrier that, in our experience, receives far too little attention but is really responsible for most resistance to change. Even if people see the new right thing, they must also see a way to travel from doing the right thing poorly to doing it well. How to paint inspiring and illuminating new visions, as well as promising paths to the promised land, fills the next chapter.

5

THE KEYS TO MOVING: DESTINATIONS, RESOURCES, AND REWARDS

When we last left you as CEO of QuadQ, you had successfully created sufficient contrast and confrontation for people to see that the old strategic map was just plain wrong, and you had painted a clear picture of the new destination. However, the clearer you made the vision, the more QuadQ's people resisted moving to make the change. After reading the previous chapter, you now understand why. Your people know that traveling to the new destination will require that they stop doing the *wrong* thing quite competently and start doing the *right* thing quite incompetently. Now they must not only *see* the new destination, but you must help them *believe* in a path that will take them from doing the right thing poorly to doing it well. Without this fundamental belief in a path and their individual abilities to follow it, your people will refuse to move—despite an obvious and compelling destination.

BELIEVING

Helping others to gain this belief requires three straightforward steps:

1. Make sure others see the destination or target clearly.

2. Give them the skills, resources, and tools (the gear) to reach the destination.

3. Deliver valuable rewards along the journey.

These steps emerge from one of the most tested and validated theories in human psychology and management—expectancy theory. Although we do not want to waste your time with the detailed ins and outs of the theory, we mention it for two reasons. First, what we present is not just our thoughts or opinions but is supported by scores of published research studies. Second, although we generated many ideas for this book, we do not want credit where it is not due. As PhD students, we studied under one of the principal architects of expectancy theory. Put simply, we know that expectancy theory is not our idea; yet it has powerful application in overcoming the second gravitational force and barrier to change—failure to move.

STEP 1: DESTINATION

Just imagine how motivated you are to shoot at an unclear target or take off after a fuzzy destination. If the destination is not clear, what is the chance of arriving there? If the chance of arriving is low, how high is your motivation to try? The answers to these questions are obvious. If the direction and destination are not clear, your motivation to move forward is nil. As a consequence, it is no surprise that over 100 research studies have confirmed this.

What may surprise you is how often leaders think the new right thing is crystal clear but subordinates report that both the direction and the destination are like a fog. If it is so critical (and obvious) that they must be clear, why do leaders fail to make them clear? Once again, are we brain dead or what? Our explanation reverts to the "I get it" mistake. Precisely because we see where we're headed clearly, we think everyone else sees it as clearly. What we must keep in mind is that seeing the destination clearly as leaders means absolutely *nothing* to followers. The only thing that matters, the only thing that motivates our employees, is whether *they* see it clearly.

Consequently, Step 1 is all about checking how clearly *others* see where they are going. This assumes that we have tried to clarify the destination. (And making that clear to ourselves as the leaders of change is Step 0. If we haven't done that, it's time to start over with Remedial Leadership 101—defining the destination.)

How do you do Step 1? How do you check to see how clearly others see the new direction? You can't use people's resistance to move as an indicator. As we have explained, people might not move because where they need to go *is not* clear, but, ironically, they might also resist moving because the destination *is* in fact very clear. Consequently, people's failure to move really gives you no insight as to whether or not they see the destination clearly. What, then, can you do? How can you determine whether the destination looks clear or fuzzy to others?

The easiest way is to ask people to do what *you* have already done. Here's what we mean. As a leader, you have already produced verbal and visual images of the old and new strategic map. Ask your people directly and indirectly to describe (or literally draw) each key element of the new map. If they can't do it, the strategic map and its key components are not clear; people don't know where they are going.

If they can draw or articulate the old and new maps, take one more step for travel insurance. Ask them what the new destination will require from them in terms of personal capabilities. If the old map involved walking along the beach and the new one requires trekking up a mountain, anyone who sees the difference will surely recognize the need for boots on the mountain trek, whereas bare feet might have been perfectly fine for the beach.

For example, the CEO of a large energy company laid out a new strategic map that demanded a shift from independent and autonomous business units to more interdependent and coordinated units. If her vision was clear enough, company executives should be able to communicate back to the CEO a solid grasp of how all the firm's value chain activities fit together and the importance of effective conflict-resolution skills as required capabilities for following the new strategic map successfully. If the CEO's direct reports can't see some of these key capabilities on their own, odds are that the target is not yet clear enough.

Unlike the university professor who requires students simply to regurgitate what they have heard, checking for understanding pushes us to see whether others see the new map clearly enough that *they* can describe it. If their description of the destination is close enough to what's in your mind, you can feel reasonably comfortable that the direction and destination are adequately clear to them.

For complete comfort though, people should not only describe the destination, but should also speculate about its possible implications. The point here is not to test whether the implications they see are identical to yours. Instead, the point is to check and see whether others can see clearly enough where they are going for *them* to perceive reasonable implications of the next steps to take along the path of change.

STEP 2: RESOURCES

Once the destination is clear in employees' minds, the key question then becomes whether people believe they have what it takes to walk the path and reach the promised-land. Scaling a tall peak sounds great, unless you don't believe you have the necessary gear (ropes, boots, harnesses, etc.), the required skills, or the mandated physical strength. Quite simply, if people believe they really *can* walk the path and reach the destination, they are much more motivated to try. If they do not believe, they will not try. But once again, what idiot leader among us would ask employees to scale a mountain for which they have neither the necessary gear nor capabilities? By definition, if we give them a mountain to climb, we believe they have what it takes to make it.

Similar to Step 1, the key to Step 2 lies in realizing that *our* assessments do not matter. In the final analysis, *it is what employees believe that counts*. If they do not believe, they will not try (or at least will not try very hard or for very long). If they do believe, they will persist. Although we as leaders must make our assessments as to what the required tools and capabilities are, the real challenge centers on determining whether employees believe they possess what it takes and helping them to believe if they do not.

A brief personal example is valuable here. Several years ago, Stewart managed a consulting firm in Japan. In that position, one of Stewart's responsibilities was a new product launch. He made the destination clear to the salesmen. They all clearly saw the sales target. Stewart then put together a compelling reward package. Salesmen saw the target clearly and wanted the promised rewards, yet the launch went nowhere—no sales prospects emerged.

Why? In some private conversations after work, Stewart was told that none of the salesmen had mentioned the new product to a single client. Generally, no mention of the new product produces no sales prospects. Why wasn't the product mentioned? Because the salesmen were adept at their jobs, they imagined how a sales call might go—what they would say, what a client might ask, how they would answer, etc. In so doing, they all saw that clients might ask a few questions for which they did not have answers. That would be embarrassing—which was unacceptable in a Japanese context. To avoid potential embarrassment, the salesmen simply avoided the situation by not mentioning the new product.

What was missing? The destination was clear. The rewards were motivating. The salesmen had the selling capabilities. The resource they lacked was a bit of knowledge required to answer some tough questions. Stewart thought they had this knowledge. (To be honest, he thought he had provided it in the sales meeting—clearly a victim of the "I get it" trap.) Stewart did not check to see that the salesmen believed they had the knowledge. All it took was their believing that they did *not* have the resource (i.e., knowledge that would answer certain customer questions), and they didn't even attempt to make the trip down this new product path, despite it being clear and highly rewarded.

How do you determine whether people who believe in the path also believe that they can follow it with success? Clearly, the first step requires a determination of what the critical resources are. If the future path to company success is integrated customer solutions, for example, you must determine what core capabilities are required to walk that path successfully. If integrated solutions demand effective cross-functional teamwork, people must believe they have those capabilities. Keep in mind that the clearer the path, the easier it is for people to see what is required to walk it successfully and, therefore, the easier it is to decide whether they have or lack the gear or capabilities to follow the path. If they don't believe they possess them, they stay put.

The first move down the path regarding resources is determining what you believe are the resources required to arrive at the new destination. The next move is assessing whether employees believe they have the required resources (skills, knowledge, tools, manpower, etc.). The third move is providing any missing required resources, including building capabilities in your people—if they do not currently have them. This may take substantial training, education, experience, mentoring, coaching, or any number of other techniques to generate the essential capabilities for mastering the new right things required in your change initiative.

In summary, regarding resources, employees essentially ask the question, If I try, can I do it? If the answer is no (no matter how clear the target), people will fail to move. They need to believe they have the right resources—the skills, knowledge, hardware, software, tools, manpower, capabilities, etc.—to do make the trek.

STEP 3: REWARDS

Step 1 ensured that the destination is clear in employees' minds, and Step 2 formed a belief in employees that they had the resources to walk the path and reach the promised-land. Now Step 3 relies on the most overused and, as a result, the most familiar aspect of getting people to move—reward. All of us know the power of rewards in motivating and moving people. In any change initiative, employees will believe in the path that leads from doing the right thing poorly to doing it well in part *if* they believe that walking the path will be rewarding.

When we think of reward, many of us think of money. No question, money can motivate employees. However, it is not the only motivating reward, and it is not nearly as powerful as we often suppose. To put money in its proper place as a reward, we must appreciate two important things.

First, money often represents a means to something else that people care about. Money buys a new car when the old one breaks down. Money also buys a new car that can boost one's ego. Money buys a college education for a child. Money buys a vacation to take a break from earning more money. For many people, money is a necessary means to what they truly value— security, ego, status, friendship, health, fun. However, as we discover what people really care about, we may also identify alternative means (instead of money) to fulfill those needs. For example, employees who are driven by status may find a visible assignment much more rewarding than money. For people who really value fun, a company party may deliver the goods. The point is that many things matter much more to people than money, and money is often just a means to what really matters to them, anyway. If we can identify what others truly desire, we may well take a different (and often more direct) route to help them fulfill it.

The second thing to keep in mind about money is that its effects are often much less powerful than we believe. For example, a yearly bonus (if it is large enough) can be a very powerful incentive for most people. Yet if the daily reinforcement employees receive from peers and leaders contradicts the incentive scheme underlying the yearly bonus, which reward will exert more power? You may find it surprising, but research has clearly established that, in most cases, the immediate and repeated reinforcements people receive are much more powerful than once-yearly bonuses. The point here is not to abolish annual bonuses but simply to recognize that bonuses paid out more frequently, along with daily praise, recognition, compliments, and so on, are much more compelling reinforcements than once-yearly experiences.

How do you figure out what people really value? Do you just go up to them and ask, "Hey, what do you really value? Tell me so that I can put it in place and make sure that you believe in this new destination and actually start moving?" Of course you don't. Although we think we have a framework to help you investigate what people value, there is no shortcut or "one-minute" solution here. People are not human vending machines with personal values prominently displayed for any prospective bidder inserting the right coins and pushing the right buttons. Instead, to discover what others deeply value and care about demands significant time and sincere effort. Period.

People can value almost anything. If you used the process of elimination, it might take decades to eliminate all the secondary and tertiary values and zero in on a person's core values. If you want to come in out of the cold to understand others' motivation, consider the ARCTIC approach (achievement, relations, conceptual/thinking, improvement, and control).

The ARCTIC approach encompasses major categories of values (some scholars call them *needs*) that people exhibit from a motivational perspective. Each one has two related sub-dimensions, as summarized in the following:

Achievement.

- **Accomplishment:** The need to meet or beat goals, to do better in the future than one has done in the past.
- **Competition:** The need to compare one's performance with that of others and do better than others do.

Relations.

- **Approval:** The need to be appreciated and recognized by others.
- **Belonging:** The need to feel a part of and accepted by the group.

Conceptual/Thinking.

- **Problem Solving:** The need to confront problems and create answers.
- **Coordination:** The need to relate pieces and integrate them into a whole.

Improvement.

- **Growth:** The need to feel continued improvement and growth as a person, not just improved results.
- **Exploration:** The need to move into unknown territory for discovery.

Control.

- **Competence:** The need to feel personally capable and competent.
- **Influence:** The need to influence others' opinions and actions.

Although we may all exhibit these needs or values to some extent or another, research clearly demonstrates, and no doubt your own personal experience verifies, that the strength of these needs varies from person to person. Why they vary is the subject of countless books and debates. That question is really not relevant here. What is important is that if we want to move people to a new destination, we must ensure that the prize for following the new path is motivating to each individual.

Consider just one short sentence uttered by Stewart and see whether you can zero in on what motivates him. As the 2002 Winter Olympics approached, Stewart commented, "Well at least I can still out-ski both my older boys [ages 19 and 14]." Using the ARCTIC framework, what motivates Stewart? If you look back through the list, one item jumps out more than the others—achievement and, in particular, competition. The point here is that listening carefully to others provides a constant stream of clues as to what they really care about and, therefore, what you can use to really motivate them.

For some, the motivating prize is an opportunity to explore. For others, highlighting exploration would simply paralyze them with fear, and instead, we might stress the personal growth opportunities that a new path presents. The key is listening and identifying the most powerful motivators for a given individual.

Astute readers who face large-scale change initiatives will no doubt be thinking, "This is all well and good, but I have hundreds of people I need to get moving. I can't afford to get to know them all and provide customized, individual rewards." Moving many people at once is a challenge, but our point is that if you cannot get individuals moving, the masses won't, either. The trick is to cascade this individualization of understanding and reward customization down the organization. You learn what your people really value and customize the prizes you pass out for following the path to change. Then your direct delegates do the same and customize rewards for their people, and so on down the line.

By the way, the higher you are in your organization, being able to motivate individuals actually becomes even more important in making change happen. Here's why. Typically, the higher we ascend in the organizational hierarchy, the more convinced we often become of our power and authority. After all, as CEOs or senior executives, when we call people, they get right back to us; people change calendars to meet our schedule; when we shout "Jump!" people ask "How high?" on the way up. However, keep in mind that the higher you go up the organization, the more people outnumber you down the organization. No matter what you declare to shareholders or the media about a marvelous new strategic initiative, if all those people below you don't move individually, the entire organization doesn't move, either, and then you are left with unfulfilled promises and disappointed shareholders.

PULLING IT ALL TOGETHER

Successfully getting people to move encompasses several key points. First, people fail to see the need for change because the mental maps already in their heads blind them. If you can't change these maps, change goes nowhere. However, even if you get people to recognize that what was once right is now wrong, they still may not move. In other words, although overcoming the initial force of gravity and breaking through the first barrier to change is necessary, it is not sufficient. Change initiatives can and often do fail because people fail to move, even when they see the need. And they fail to move because they do not see or believe in (1) the new path, (2) their ability to walk it, or (3) the rewarding outcomes of the journey and destination. Consequently, they prefer sticking with competence at doing the wrong thing in lieu of incompetence at doing the right one.

For people to really get moving, they must clearly see in their own minds—not yours—where they are going. They must *believe* they have the required resources to walk the path and reach the promised-land. And they must believe that outcomes *they* value will result from following the path outlined by the new map and reaching the destination. The key thing to remember here is that *their* belief that all three components are in place counts—*not yours*. If they don't see it and believe it, nothing else really matters.

We wish this were the end of the story, but it isn't, quite yet. In the next chapter we examine why, despite seeing and believing, many people still fail to finish the task of change.

6

BRAIN BARRIER #3: FAILURE TO FINISH

Returning to our flight metaphor, at this point, you have pushed the throttle forward, and your hundred-ton strategic change project begins to lumber down the runway. You build up speed until you reach the point where people recognize that the old right thing is now wrong. You continue to build momentum until you pass the critical point where you need more runway to stop than to take off. People now see what the new right thing is. You celebrate a little; you have overcome the initial gravitational forces and broken through the first barrier of change.

As you continue down the runway, your airspeed climbs until you reach that magical point of "rotation," where the plane's speed is sufficient to pull back on the wheel and lift the nose up. Then the friction and noise of the tires on the tarmac disappear as you break free from the earth. Now people not only see the new right thing, but they believe in the path that will enable them to go from doing the new right thing poorly to doing it well. You celebrate a bit more; you have broken through the second barrier of change. You are airborne.

Given all the energy it takes to get off the ground, it should be smooth flying from here, right? By some rules of fairness, it should be, but anyone with any experience in leading strategic change knows that some of the toughest aspects of change are yet to come. Like a plane, where dashing down the runway and then lifting off are necessary for flight, all it takes is a bit of a throttle back on the power, and the plane will come crashing back to the ground. Despite breaking the bonds of earth, gravity still exerts its invisible power, waiting for the opportunity to pull flights of fancy back into its crushing embrace.

Thus, even after overcoming the initial force of gravity and breaking through the first two barriers of change—i.e., failure to see and failure to move—the third brain barrier remains: the failure to finish. This force silently, patiently, and persistently waits for any opportunity to demonstrate its ruining power. Consequently, successful change must also overcome the third barrier of failure to finish—not going far or fast enough.

Whether the focus of the transformation is on quality, innovation, customer service, speed, or globalization, the full impact and benefits of the "organizational" change cannot be realized until the majority of "individuals" change. Quite simply, new transformational strategies do not make a difference until people think and act differently. Historically, as we have already pointed out, people do not change easily or quickly. When you have an organizational change that involves thousands of individuals, it is impossible to implement the change overnight; instead, it takes months and months, if not years. It takes time for the desired changes to ripple through the organization. As a consequence of this time lag, there is a significant risk that people will get tired and lost during the interim. These are the two principal forces that hold organizations back from moving fast enough or going far enough in their change—people getting tired and people getting lost.

GETTING TIRED

People get tired because organizational transformation is fundamentally not about transforming the organization; it is about transforming the people who work in it. Certain aspects of the organization—its strategy, structure, or systems—can and often need to be transformed. However, have you ever seen a transformational strategy make a long-term difference when the individuals in the company did not have to transform their thinking and behavior? Have you ever seen a new structure work when the people in that structure did not change their thoughts and actions? The answer is no. The "rubber" of change meets the "road" of results in people's behaviors. If the people themselves don't change, the wheels spin, and the strategic initiative gets zero traction.

For example, an airline can decide that its new strategy and culture will focus on putting the customer first, as British Airlines (BA) did a few years ago. BA even implemented a program called *Customer 1st*. BA can create a new mission statement; it can put out a thousand press releases; it can put up a million Customer 1st banners in airports all around the world; but customers experience and respond to the change only when ticket agents, reservation agents, flight attendants, ground personnel, etc. actually put the customer first. Until then, it is all just corporate peacock feathers.

This is not to say that organizational elements, such as incentives or information systems, do not have an impact on people and their behaviors. Clearly, they can and do. For example, people act on the information they have, so information systems matter because of the type, quality, and speed of information they deliver to people. The point is not to say that systems do not matter. Rather, in the final analysis, what really matters in organizational transformations is the change in people's behaviors and how systems either enhance or detract from that.

Unfortunately, too often this simple fundamental is forgotten, or at least temporarily lost, in the system focus of the moment. In one sense, this is understandable. How can a senior executive reach out and change 100,000 employees? How can a department manager reach out and transform even 40 people? It is hard to conceive of changing individuals, so we naturally reach out and try to pull one or two organizational levers, which we hope in turn will change the individuals. We reach out for the incentive lever or the organizational structure lever. We do this for a good reason. These levers do have an impact on people. Unfortunately, far too often their impact is less than we imagine or hope.

Over the last 50 years, research has consistently demonstrated that, to employees, organizational elements such as strategy, structure, or even compensation and incentive systems are abstract and remote. In contrast, the example they see in their bosses, the reinforcement they get from their peers, or the punishment they get from customers is much closer—it is "proximate," in academic speak. Research further demonstrates that proximate factors drive people's behaviors significantly more than do distant factors.

This is one of the reasons why transformation levers such as "reorganization" do not produce the results most executives hope for. This disappointment and our inability to see the limitations of new organizational charts in transforming people are partly why we see reorganization after reorganization. In many firms, it looks as though executives never graduated from the childhood game of musical chairs. These executives seem to have forgotten (or perhaps never really understood) that a new organizational chart has an impact only when individual people on the charts behave differently. If the boxes and reporting lines change but the attitudes and behaviors remain, so do the results.

But just to make sure that there is no misunderstanding, let us say again that changing strategies, structures, or systems is important to transformations. However, they are not *the* transformation. At best, they are catalysts and facilitators. The problem is that, in too many cases, executives view these valuable means as the ends. Once the strategy, structure, or system is changed, they think the job is done and that "the rest will naturally happen." Nothing could be further from the truth. The crux of success or, in other words, the key to overcoming the failure to finish, lies in changing a large number of individuals, not in pulling organizational levers.

Unfortunately, changing individuals is not easy, especially if the change required is dramatic. Gravity is a powerful opponent. Consider that a plane flying across the Atlantic Ocean will burn one-third of its fuel just taking off and getting to cruise altitude.

Changing people is no different. Tremendous energy and effort are required to get people to change.

As we discussed earlier in the book, people are programmed to survive and, as a consequence, naturally stick with what has worked, what has proven successful. Most people do not walk by faith. Most people wisely live by the philosophy of *seeing is believing*. If they did not, they would follow any wild, unproven, idiotic idea that came along. In fact, many employees believe that to be what is wrong with senior managers. Employees call it *management by best seller*. Too many managers simply grab onto the latest best-selling idea without really knowing whether it will work.

Employees are wise to walk in the proven paths of successful maps. In that wisdom, they resist changes based on whims; they believe in and stick with what they have seen work with their own eyes. The gravity and pull of their previous ways of thinking and behaving exert a constant and massive force. In contrast, to employees, a new destination and path seem to require letting go of gravity, floating in the air, and walking by faith. For most, faith is not an easy concept. As evidence, just ask any clergy, priest, pastor, monk, or rabbi. Trying to get at least some people to change from "seeing is believing" to "believing is seeing" is hard work. A mission statement does not do it. A new organizational chart will not cut it. Faith is not about words or boxes and lines. Faith is about trust.

Employees ask themselves, "Do I trust the promised outcomes? Do I trust my own ability to behave in new ways and achieve the desired results? Do I trust that if I put in all this time and effort to walk this path, the rug will not be yanked out from under me, and a new strategy, structure, and system will be announced just as I'm getting the hang of things?"

If you are trying to get employees to think and behave differently, their willingness initially to walk by faith is a function of how much they trust you. If they trust you, they will venture forth. If they do not, they will not.

Although this is true, it is beginning to sound a bit philosophical, so let's bring it down to a concrete and practical level. Consider the case of an airline gate agent, Sam, working for Your Average Airline (YAA). As the name implies, YAA is not bad but is not particularly good at customer service. However, the new CEO has announced that YAA plans to win the competitive battle by putting the customer first. He even names the new strategy and change program *Customer 1st*. (The CEO did this, of course, after making sure that BA had not trademarked the phrase.)

Sam listens to the CEO's presentation about why treating customers badly destroys loyalty and hurts organizational performance. Sam pays careful attention to the arguments about why putting the customer first will differentiate YAA and lead customers to fly YAA more often. He even listens closely enough to see that with more loyal customers and higher occupancy (*load factors* in the CEO's lingo), the company will make more money, and as a consequence, Sam will have a more secure and brighter future. Sam begins to accept the new map and destination—the land of Customer 1st. He begins to alter his mental terrain.

YAA's new CEO, being brighter than most, presents a clear picture not only for *why* putting the customer first is a great idea, but also for *how* Sam can achieve it. He is provided the required resources. Sam is given training about how to handle customer complaints at the gate and how to speak in a tone that comes across more pleasantly to customers. The path to the land of Customer 1st begins to come into clearer focus. Sam begins to see not only the destination, but also the path that could lead there. Why doesn't Sam at this point just take off running down the path without a moment's reflection in his rearview mirror?

Sam, like all workers, is smart. He does not act on simple blind faith. Instead, he acts on what he believes will give him the best return for his investment. He almost unconsciously makes comparisons between the ratio of effort and reward of the old with the anticipated effort/reward ratio of the new.

In the past, it took little effort for Sam to put the customer second, third, or even tenth. In fact, it was quite easy *not* to be *customer-centric* (one of the other key buzzwords used in the Customer 1st training program Sam attended). Up to this point, Sam has had little trouble being Sam-centric.

For example, a customer recently came running up to the gate, completely out of breath, but still shouting, "I need to get on that plane." The plane was still at the gate, but the final passenger count was completed, and the door was about to be closed. Sam was tired and didn't feel like being particularly pleasant. It took little effort to say in a fairly unsympathetic tone, "I'm sorry, boarding is closed." The customer challenged, "What do you mean, closed? I'm late because of a stupid mechanical problem on one of your other flights. Besides, I can see the plane. It's still at the gate." Without any effort, Sam replied, "As I said, boarding is closed." It also didn't take much effort to tune out the passenger's ravings that followed. Sam simply walked away. Sam's effort and investment were low.

What about the benefits—the return on his investment? Surely Sam could *not* have liked the ranting and ravings of the irate customer. True, he did not. However, the ranting and raving were not all that negative for Sam, partly because Sam had become quite skilled at tuning them out over time. What were the positive rewards of being Sam-centric, rather than customer-centric? Power and control. The customer did not get on the plane for one simple reason—because Sam said so. In Sam's book, that was not a bad outcome at all. In fact, it felt pretty good. For one brief moment, Sam had the destiny (or at least the destination) of the customer in his hands. When it came to looking for a good effort/outcome ratio, Sam did not have to walk by faith. He knew from experience that what he already had was good. One ounce of effort (I'm sorry, boarding is closed)—three pounds of reward (I control your life).

Now consider the same situation but with the new customer orientation. Assuming that the customer arrives late enough that it is not within Sam's authority to get him on the plane, Sam still has to turn down the customer. However, the new Customer 1st strategy asks him to put much more effort into both the words and tone he uses. The customer still shouts, "I need to get on that plane." Sam still has to say, "I'm sorry, but boarding is closed." But this time he also has to work hard to convey a tone of understanding and sympathy. The customer still challenges, "What do you mean closed? I'm late because of a stupid mechanical problem on one of your other flights. Besides, I can see the plane. It's still at the gate." Now the new investments required by the new strategic map start to pile up. Sam has to think into the customer's situation and convey even greater sympathy. Sam has to think, "I can understand this customer's frustration. Anyone would be frustrated in his shoes."

Still, sympathy alone is not enough. The new organizational transformation requires more. Whereas before, Sam could have just tuned out the customer, now he must put significantly more effort into solving the customer's problem. To do this well, Sam needs to know what other flights on YAA will get the customer to his destination and what flights on alternative airlines might also work. In the same instant that Sam must process this information, he also needs to say something such as, "I can imagine how frustrating the situation is, and I will do whatever I can to help you get to San Diego. We have another flight in 90 minutes that I think I can get you on. I may even be able to upgrade you."

For all his extra investment of attitude and energy, what does Sam get? At first, he is not sure. The first time he tries this new approach, he has to walk by the faith he puts in the trainer's or his boss's promise. Sam is hoping for the smile and "thank you" that had been promised, but what does he get? The first time he tries this new approach, he gets a customer who fires back, "I don't care about an upgrade or leaving later, I need to get on *that* plane. What part of *that* plane don't you understand?"

At this point, Sam is tempted to retaliate, but instead, he exercises even more faith in the new destination and path, saying, "I appreciate your frustration, but as I said, I can get you on our next flight to San Diego." Eventually, the customer relents and agrees to go on a later flight. He even manages a "thank you" before stomping off.

Unconsciously, Sam compares the return on investment ratios (ROIs) of the old and the new. The old way: not much effort and a nice reward of feeling powerful. The new way: lots of effort and not that much reward. Should Sam continue to have faith that the rewards will improve, that customers will smile and thank him over time? Should he continue to believe that eventually their smiles and thanks will translate into better performance for the company and a more secure and rewarding future for him?

Unfortunately, Sam is alone in his thoughts. There was no one else at the gate during the encounter—no boss, no peer. No one was around to say, "Nice job." No one was there to encourage him to have faith and hang in there.

Repeat this one scene over and over again, and it is easy to see why Sam gets tired (Exhibit 6-1). If Sam gets tired, it is easy to see how the gravitational pull of Sam's old mental map could overpower the initial momentum of the new. Multiply Sam by several hundred other similar gate agents, and it is easy to see why the new Customer 1st strategy might not transform the organization or its results.

In sum, change efforts fail to finish because people get tired. They get tired in an absolute sense because change requires

Sam

EXHIBIT 6-1
Failure to finish: Getting tired.

energy and effort. The more substantial the change, the more energy and effort must be expended in targeting change in individual employees. More important than the absolute level of energy required is the tiredness that comes from the effort of walking a new path that seems to provide an inferior ROI to an individual employee. Employees get tired of walking by the vapor of faith when the concreteness of the past has worked and would continue to work just fine, from their perspective.

GETTING LOST

Because major transformations of people and organizations are long journeys, people not only get tired along the way, they can also get lost—very lost. Over the long transformational journey, they lose track of where they started, where they are, and where that places them in relation to where they thought they wanted to be and go. Once all this uncertainty sets in and employees feel lost, pressing ahead is not very compelling.

To understand this, we need only return to Sam, our gate agent. When we last left Sam, he was getting tired. It took lots of extra effort to put customers first. In many cases, that extra effort was not yielding extra benefits. Fortunately for YAA, Sam was willing to walk a bit more by faith than the average person. Sam knows from past experiences that seeing usually is believing, but sometimes believing is seeing. He knows that sometimes, you see something only after you first believe in it. He trusts you—his boss—which makes it easier to have faith in the future. Consequently, he persists in his Customer 1st efforts. He gets some encouragement from you, and he pays special attention to peers, who also seem to be trying. Sam tries to ignore those colleagues who have only bad things to say about the whole Customer 1st notion.

Six months go by. Sam has been working on being more sympathetic, using the phrases he was taught, and solving customer problems more efficiently and effectively. He feels as though he has made some progress, but how much? He is not sure. "What about the rest of the organization?" he wonders. "Are they working as hard as I am?" In his immediate work group, Sam knows that he is in the minority. Most of the others are not really taking this Customer 1st thing all that seriously. "Is his work group typical, or are most of the other groups moving down the path? Has any of his effort made any difference to customers? Have the collective efforts made any difference? Are load factors up? Are customer satisfaction levels up?" Sam just doesn't know where things stand. He is starting to feel lost (Exhibit 6-2), in which case, why should he keep moving forward?

As Sam's questions suggest, he is concerned both about his personal position and that of the company. He wants to know how far he has come personally. He has a sense that he has made progress, but he is not sure how much distance he has covered and how much more remains. He also wants to know how far the company has come. Sam does not want to be the only one who is putting in all this extra effort. He knows that many of the per-

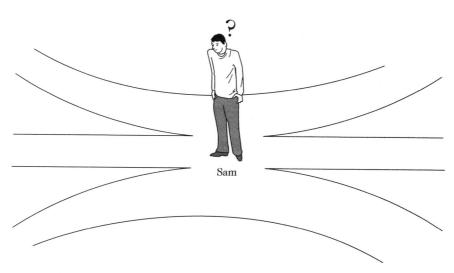

EXHIBIT 6-2
Failure to finish: Feeling lost.

sonal benefits (a more secure future) depend on organizational benefits (better financial performance) and that he alone cannot bring about the desired organizational results. If others are not doing what he is doing, if others have not made the progress he has made, Sam has no hope of seeing the benefits in which he has believed and trusted.

Unfortunately, in YAA no baseline measure was ever taken of customer satisfaction with Sam's behavior. Neither Sam nor you (his boss) really know how unhappy or happy customers were with Sam before the new strategy got underway. Perhaps more unfortunately still is that no measure has been taken since. Sam feels like fewer customers stomp away unhappy and more customers smile and thank him, but the changes have been so small over so many days that the difference is hard to see.

At the corporate level of YAA, though, there were some baseline measures. For example, corporate had measures of complaints per thousand customers before the transformation. In fact, ranking as one of the worst airlines on this measure was a key driver for the strategic change. Since implementing the change, company executives have tracked customer complaints per thousand over the last several months. They also have been able to track the level of repeat business from frequent fliers as one important measure of customer satisfaction. Finally, senior management even had an outside consulting firm conduct some customer satisfaction surveys early in the program, as well as more recently.

Not surprisingly, the results were mixed. YAA was making progress. The number of complaints per thousand was down significantly. YAA had moved from last to fifth best on this measure. However, customer satisfaction was actually down. The consultants explained that this was largely a function of raised expectations. Before the transformation, YAA customers had little reason to expect good treatment. With the launch of Customer 1st and the resulting media attention, customers' expectations went up. Although YAA employees behaviors toward customers improved, they did not improve as fast as expectations, and as a consequence, customer satisfaction scores actually dropped.

Executives of YAA worried that disseminating this and other information presented too many risks. What if competitors acquired this privileged information? What if employees got disheartened by the drop in customer scores and were too unsophisticated to appreciate the explanation? What if someone leaked this information to the media? These and a hundred other questions like them kept YAA's executives from letting anyone know how things were actually going.

As Sam's boss, you've heard rumors about how things are going, but no one has shared any concrete numbers with you. When Sam asks about progress, you can say only that you have not heard anything official. When Sam asks about his progress, what do you say? You tried telling him that he is doing fine, but he did not seem satisfied and wanted to know what specifically was going well and what he should work on. Your comment "just keep up the good work" did *not* put a smile on Sam's face.

Is it little wonder that Sam is not only a bit tired, but is feeling lost, as well? If this were a physical trek through the wilderness, how long would we expect Sam to keep going if he was unsure of where he was, the progress he had made, or how much farther it was to where he wanted to go?

Even after getting employees to see that the old right thing is now wrong and to recognize what the new right thing is, and even after getting them to believe in the path that will take them from doing the new right thing poorly to doing it well, change efforts often falter. They falter because people get tired and lost and, therefore, fail to finish. They do not go far or fast enough. Those at the controls fail to apply the right power and thrust after takeoff, and gravity is there to pull the flight of fancy crashing back to earth.

OVERCOMING THE FINAL BRAIN BARRIER

The next chapter, Chapter 7, outlines the keys to overcoming this third and final brain barrier. Without this knowledge—even though a change project has broken through the barriers of seeing and believing—there is little hope of achieving a lasting change.

Once Chapter 7 has laid out these key steps, Chapter 8 walks back through the principles and applies them to the challenge of changing to greater growth. With the model firmly in place and integrated with the challenge of growth, Chapters 9, 10, and 11 provide a pragmatic toolkit for leading strategic change.

7

THE KEYS TO FINISHING: CHAMPIONS AND CHARTING

G iven all the time and energy it takes to overcome the first two brain barriers and get people to see and believe, it is sometimes heartbreaking to see all that success go down in flames because of a failure to finish. As we explained in the last chapter, failure to finish is primarily a function of people getting tired or getting lost. These are what keep people from moving fast or far enough to achieve success. The keys to achieving success in this final stage of change are *champions* and *charting*.

PROVIDING CHAMPIONS

Remember how tired Sam, our gate agent with YAA, got even after he saw and believed in the Customer 1st change? He planted the seed of Customer 1st in his behavior, but like all seeds, it did not sprout immediately or grow into full bloom overnight. It needed consistent care and nurturing. Like a seed, it needed the most attention when it was young. Sam's first few experiments with the new Customer 1st behavior were the most critical. That is when the seed was the most vulnerable. Deny it a bit of water just after it is planted, and it has a good chance of dying.

YAA was lucky to get Sam to try the experiment, given that the rewards were by no means assured. Where was the champion to help nurture, water, and feed this new seed? It would be just plain dumb to expect Sam to play champion to himself. Without a champion, Sam will tire, slow down his attempts to change, and likely quit far short of the goal.

The point of coming back to this example is that, normally when we talk about "change champions," audiences and readers alike almost always think we're talking about high people in powerful positions. This again is Remedial Leadership 101. Of course, senior executives must be champions of large-scale organizational changes. Organizational transformation efforts that lack committed executives will fail. However, we have interviewed dozens of senior executives who have supported and "championed" change efforts that have fallen flat. The reason for referring back to our example of Sam is to illustrate that, without champions close to the action, the champions in the executive suite matter very little and on their own cannot bring about lasting change. The change champions we are talking about are on the line—not in the executive suite.

Just imagine again for a moment Sam's first experiment with Customer 1st. Do you think that Sam is influenced by the fact that the CEO is 110% a champion for the Customer 1st change when the customer is yelling in Sam's face, "What is it about *that* plane that you don't understand?" The answer is *no*. Sam does not care at that moment about the CEO. Yet that moment with the customer is the moment of truth. That moment when Sam exercises some faith, plants the seed, and waits for the results is when a champion is needed—not days before or after. That is the place where the champion needs to be, not on the 27th floor in the cherry wood-paneled executive suite. The champion is needed next to the action when it happens—where the rubber meets the road.

It is a given that senior executives support the change. Of course, they need to voice their support repeatedly. However, they need to manifest their support by ensuring that there are champions of the change at the point and time in which the early walks by faith occur. Unless the senior executives do this, all their video, PowerPoint, broadband, radio, and closed-circuit TV presentations are nothing more than tinkling cymbals of the top brass.

For a large-scale change effort, it may not be practical or possible to put in place the required number of champions (let alone quality) to ensure that all the early walks of faith are supported and reinforced, that all the early seeds that are planted are fed and watered. In these cases, it is critical to identify and designate some early launch sites. They should be called *launch sites*, not *pilots* or *test cases*, or anything else that can leave people wondering about executive commitment to the change. These early launch sites should be staffed with trained and motivated champions who will be next to the action when it happens. Only in this way can you have a chance to break the hold of the third gravitational force of change and help employees avoid getting tired, slowing down, and giving up too early.

These champions must know what to look for and what to reinforce. They must know how to reinforce what they're looking for. Imagine again being Sam's boss. What is it you are looking for? Are you looking for results or efforts? Initially, you are looking for efforts. Sam is not going to be good at something he has never done before, so you have to encourage his efforts, not the results. You have to stay close to the action at first so that you are in a position to make a big deal out of the first successful result. Unless you stay close to the action initially, the natural and likely negative results can easily kill the desired behavior.

At first, Sam is not going to be good at Customer 1st, scientists at QuadQ are not going to be good a working in cross-functional teams, sales people at Xerox are not going to be good at document solutions. The natural consequences that will follow these initially less than stellar capabilities on average will be negative. We don't need 60 years of research (though it's there) to tell us that, if left uncompensated, these natural and negative consequences will kill the desired, new behavior. The job of change champions is to counteract this natural force. In summary, to do this you need to (1) be close to the action, (2) look for the desired efforts—not results, and (3) counteract the natural negative consequences with positive ones.

The determination of the right positive rewards for desired efforts takes us right back to Chapter 5. There is no substitute for knowing your people and understanding what types of rewards they value. For some, it is simple praise; for others, it is highlighting that they are doing better than other employees. As we already said, there is no magic formula for determining which types of rewards you should use to encourage early change efforts—despite less than desired results. All we can offer is a framework of rewards from which you can be reasonably sure there are one or two that fit virtually any subordinate you have. Only you can discover or know which one or two are the most powerful for a given individual.

CHARTING PROGRESS

Although making sure that Sam has a champion by his side when he plants his first few Customer 1st seeds is critical (by the way the person does not have to be Sam's boss), it is not sufficient. You will recall that, after several weeks and months, Sam began to wonder how he was doing and how much progress the organization was making. Without this knowledge, he began to feel lost; feeling lost, he had little incentive to keep going.

When it comes to measuring progress, it needs to be done both at the executive suite and in the trenches. All the Sams of YAA need to know how the organization is doing. Part of their reward is tied to the organization's performance. That performance— the good, bad, and ugly—needs to be communicated. Without it, Sam is left to imagine the worst. If he imagines that progress is not being made, why should he keep going? In our experience, in 99 cases out of 100, the actual performance of the change effort, no matter how bad, is not as bad as people can imagine if left to their own devices. In the absence of information from on high, employees will imagine something 100% of the time. This is a critical point and worth repeating. People cannot and do not suspend judgment and conclusions for long. Lacking any information or conclusions from management, employees will form their own. Normally, they assume that if things were good, they would hear about it. Therefore, if they are not hearing anything, then things must be bad, really bad. The key point here is that anyone who believes that employees will over-interpret bad news and who hopes that they will simply suspend conclusions in the face of no news is mistaken and misguided.

Also, the worry that Sam and the others will not be smart or sophisticated enough to understand such complicated issues as why customer satisfaction went down even as Customer 1st behaviors increased is also misguided. If Sam is smart and sophisticated enough to understand why Customer 1st was the new right way, how did he suddenly turn dumb? If he can get the vision, he can understand the sidetracks.

In addition to organization-level measurement and communication of progress, achieving success also requires monitoring and communicating at the individual level. Sure, Sam is concerned about how the organization is doing, but he is equally and perhaps more concerned about his own progress. His boss needs either a reliable, intuitive, and informal means of measuring progress or a structured and formal one. In either case, Sam needs to know how much progress he has made. He needs to know whether that level of progress fails to meet, adequately meets, or exceeds expectations. He needs to know how much farther there is to go. He needs advice, counsel, and help on how to make further improvements. Without this "micro"-level monitoring and feedback, all the "macro"-level details in the world may not keep Sam from getting lost and giving up.

PULLING IT ALL TOGETHER

Taken together, the model we have worked through maps directly onto the framework we have used in outlining the barriers to remapping change. Consequently, if you can remember the barriers seeing, moving, and finishing, you can remember the model for effectively remapping change. It is as simple as the ABCs. However, rather than the ABCs of change, it is the *CBAs* of change. The acronym stands for *conceive, believe*, and *achieve*.

As Exhibit 7-1 illustrates, these three stages in implementing change successfully are designed to correspond with and over-come the three gravitational forces or barriers of change. To break through the first barrier, people must *conceive* the old right thing as wrong and see the new right thing. To break through the second brain barrier, people must *believe* in the path that will take them from doing the new right thing poorly to doing it well. Finally, to break through the third barrier, people must *achieve* and *know* they have achieved the desired results.

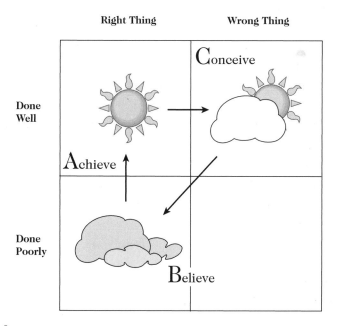

EXHIBIT 7-1
The CBAs of strategic change.

Failure to see is a function of entrenched, successful maps. The more successful they are, the more blinding they are. It takes high contrast and confrontation to break through and help employees conceive that the old right way is now wrong and to see the new vision. Heightening contrast and confrontation requires focusing on the core differences, juxtaposing their descriptions, repeating the message, and putting people in inescapable experiences to force the contrast.

Failure to move occurs because people are not motivated to go from doing the wrong thing well to doing the right thing poorly. It takes ensuring that the target is clear, that the capabilities and tools are in place, and that rewards are provided in order for employees to believe that they can go from doing the right thing poorly to doing it well.

Finally, failure to finish happens because employees get tired and lost and, therefore, do not go fast enough or far enough. Achieving success requires champions in place to reinforce and encourage the first few times the seeds of the change are planted and to applaud the first few steps in their walk of faith. It requires monitoring progress and communicating individual and collective improvement.

In combination, conceiving, believing, and knowing what you are achieving can overcome the force of gravity and allow you as a leader to break through the three critical brain barriers and redraw the maps in people's heads to create lasting change.

BREAKTHROUGH INNOVATION AND GROWTH

So far we have broken down and covered the elements of our change model separately. Although this helps highlight and clarify the specific parts and steps, in reality they need to be applied in an integrated fashion. To get a sense of how all the pieces fit together, it is helpful to walk through the entire model and all the principles focusing on a single organizational challenge. Although companies face a variety of challenges from technology to globalization and everything in between, growth is the one we find the most pressure for, both inside and outside the company. Given the focus on shareholder value these days, this is probably not surprising. Without growth to cash flow and earnings, it is virtually impossible to sustain increased returns to shareholders. Consequently, we thought it would be valuable to illustrate further the principles of the CBA change model by examining some cases of leading strategic change for growth.

CONCEIVING

Most firms we have worked with or studied, though certainly not all, report that the biggest obstacle to greater growth is getting employees (including senior executives) to see new opportunities—i.e., breaking through the first brain barrier. As we discussed at the outset of the book, people are blind to opportunities because of the light already in their eyes. In almost every case, the firm's current low growth was preceded by a period of higher growth. The longer the growth period of that industry, product, market, or technology, the more established the mental maps of where growth lies and what leads to it. The key, then, is breaking out of these restrictive mental maps.

We have found that a key to success in helping people conceive of new avenues of growth is to contrast their limited maps of present business with expansive ones of the future. One simple

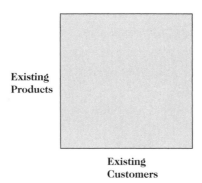

Existing
Products

Existing
Customers

EXHIBIT 8-1
The way we are.

tool we have used that works across different industries and products is illustrated here.

First, we have those involved, whether they are senior executives or factory workers, talk about the existing products and existing customers. We then place their basic descriptions of the products and customers in a box such as the one in Exhibit 8-1.

We then place this box in a larger, two-dimensional matrix, illustrated in Exhibit 8-2.

Although this matrix is not our invention and is certainly not new, we find it effective in helping people see that there is plenty of growth "space" to go after. General Electric is now the classic example of a company that has been primarily in low-growth industries but has maintained superior growth by expanding out of the existing product/existing customer box (see Exhibit 8-3). For example, when Jack Welch took the helm of GE, less than 10% of its revenue came from outside the United States. One of the ways GE enhanced its growth was to "move left"—to take its existing products to new customers around the world. As growth from expanding into this part of the matrix slowed, Mr. Welch moved the company "down" by expanding into services that leveraged existing customer relationships. For example, whereas

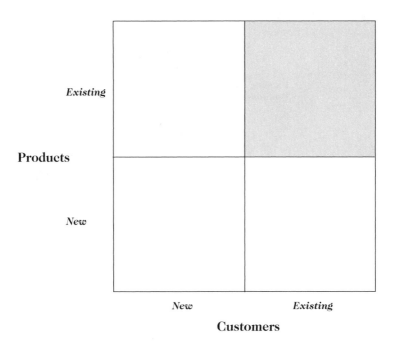

EXHIBIT 8-2
The ways we could be.

jet engine sales growth was in the single digits, moving into engine maintenance and service represented a double-digit growth opportunity.

Clearly, the lower left cell in the matrix is also an important avenue of growth. In many cases, it is the one that grabs the headlines and has been referred to as "competitive white space." However, in all honesty, as sexy as it may seem, growth from new products *and* new customers is the most challenging, not because people simply cannot see the opportunities, but also because the opportunities in this cell are generally created, not simply observed. The key: If you cannot get people to see the full matrix, you have little hope of breaking out of the existing-existing box.

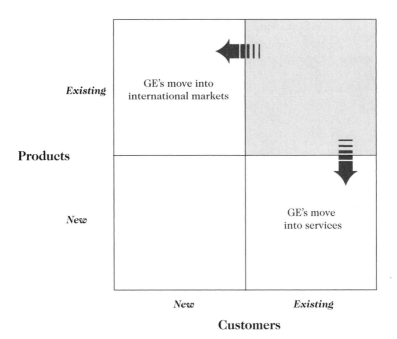

EXHIBIT 8-3
GE's growth initiatives.

As we discussed in Chapter 2, sometimes it is a matter of not just presenting a new map but also of helping people see that their old maps are not quite correct and perhaps even distorted. Earlier in the book, we talked about Kellogg's. For nearly 27 years, new ideas were in short supply at Kellogg's because of a mental map in which the existing-existing cell (i.e., existing product—cereal—and existing customer/market—United States) occupied most of the conceptual space of the growth matrix. This is why the existing-existing box also accounted for between 70% and 80% of Kellogg's revenue. In this case, the needed contrast comes by showing this distorted map against the more correct map to demonstrate that the size of growth potential outside the existing-existing space (see Exhibit 8-4).

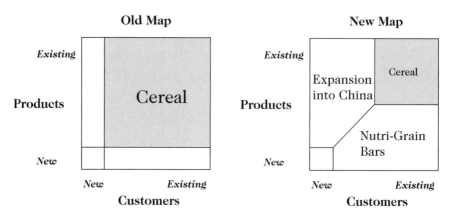

EXHIBIT 8-4
Kellogg's old and new growth maps.

In Kellogg's case, it took a new CEO to present the contrast. He not only pointed out Kellogg's failure to innovate and create new products or to expand in new markets, but highlighted the current "share of table" Kellogg's had and could potentially obtain.

Although Kellogg's historical share of the breakfast cereal market in the United States was in the 30–35% range, its share of the overall breakfast food table was significantly lower, with absolutely no presence in key food categories such as frozen breakfast foods or yogurt. Once this contrast was shown to senior executives in the late 1990s, new products were launched at a rate three times greater than in the past. Although not all have been successes, at least the old, distorted map has been replaced with a new, more accurate map. That map is moving Kellogg's in the right direction of needed innovation through new product launches, moving beyond breakfast foods altogether with a recent acquisition of Keebler Company, and continued geographic expansion throughout the world with over 30% of its current sales coming from outside the United States.

Using the simple 2x2 matrix to help people break out of the existing-existing box is important. Ensuring that the size and shape of the four cells within the matrix are not distorted is also critical to remapping people's heads for growth. However, we can step up one more level as a radical way to break the old growth maps and help people conceive new paths. This happens by transforming the previous two-dimensional matrix into a three-dimensional (3D) box (Exhibit 8-5).

Although at first the addition of the third dimension (Approach or How) may seem less important than the previous two, it can, in fact, be key to breakthrough growth. Consider Disney retail stores, for example. In 1985, Steven Burke was a young manager

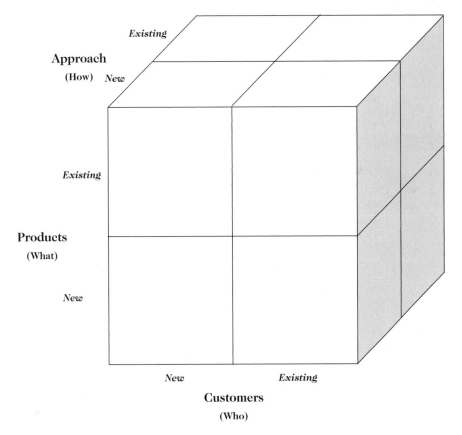

EXHIBIT 8-5
The 3D Growth Cube.

working in Disney's consumer products division. It was a poor cousin to the two main divisions of theme parks and film/television, yet Steven was charged with growth. Much of Disney's consumer products revenue came from licensing Disney characters. By the early 1980s, it seemed that every possible licensing angle had been considered. Disney characters were in books, on records, clothing, and lunch boxes, and in literally hundreds of other product categories. How could growth be expanded?

The answer came not from expanding into new products or even new customers, but in changing the way Disney got products to customers—changing the *how*. Until that time, the most concentrated sales of Disney merchandise came from stores inside Disney theme parks. Through an employee suggestion contest, an employee asked, Why do I have to go to the theme park and pay the fairly expensive entry fee to buy this wide variety of Disney merchandise? Why indeed?

From that simple question and idea came a billion-dollar business. Today, the idea of Disney stores outside of Disney theme parks seems obvious because of the pervasiveness of these stores. However, at the time, it was a radical idea. Initially, Disney stores carried virtually the same products as were merchandised in the theme parks, and the target customers were those who already knew the merchandise from their visits to the parks. In other words, initially, the growth came in the existing product/existing customer/*new* approach cell. However, it did not take long to expand out of that cell. Growth came from migrating to the left (Exhibit 8-6). In other words, growth soon came from selling existing products to not only existing customers but also to people who had never visited a Disney theme park. The retail stores then began to add products that were not carried in the park stores. In three short years, sales went from zero to over $500 million. Within five years, revenues were nearly $1 billion, and profits were double that of comparable specialty retailers.

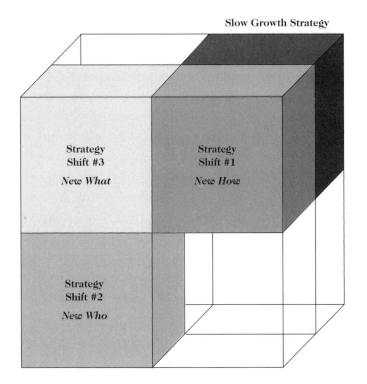

EXHIBIT 8-6
Disney Stores' 3D growth map.

Consider the case of Amazon.com. Once again, forget the crazy prices people attached to the stock and look just at the business model. Amazon.com started out selling existing books to existing book buyers. At first, all it did was change the how. It allowed people to buy books without having to leave home. This was new and, for many people, more convenient. The book business for Amazon.com went from nothing to $1 billion in sales in a few short years. Yes, we all know that Amazon.com also lost more than that during the same time period as it "invested" in the future, building better software and warehouses to ship products. Given that the pipeline for ordering was (scalable) (a new buzzword for an ancient concept called *economies of scope*), Amazon.com expanded into music, video, and electronics. Then, as we mentioned earlier in the book, it went a little crazy and expanded into virtually everything else, from lawn furniture to toys. Clearly, the market is going to force Amazon.com to focus on profits, not just growing revenues, which hit nearly $3 billion in 2000. Still, Amazon.com has grown (and some would argue too much) because it exploited the third dimension of the growth matrix—the how. It grew to a billion-dollar business primarily by selling existing products to existing customers in a new way. From there, it grew into a $3 billion business on its way to destruction or glory by adding new products to its product list and attracting new customers beyond book buyers.

Clearly, Amazon.com, like any other company, ultimately must implement and manage its growth effectively. Perhaps Amazon.com will not succeed at this challenge. Still, unless old mental maps are cracked or maybe even shattered, the journey to significant and new growth cannot begin. Amazon.com, GE, and others have begun the journey. In our experience, the key to this is confronting employees with a contrasting map that takes the one-dimensional current business and explodes it into a 3D framework of growth potential.

BELIEVING

Once you get people to conceive of growth opportunities and remap their mental terrain and how they see the potential universe of growth, not all is done. Hopefully, we have convinced you by now that, although conceiving a new map is a critical first step, it is only that—a first step. People still need to see and believe in a path that will take them from doing the new right thing poorly to doing it well.

Federal Express has seen tremendous growth from its inception in 1971. It has seen revenue increase by an average of 8% per year over the last five years. Much of that growth can be directly attributed to its hub-and-spoke business model that lets it collect packages from almost anywhere in the United States and deliver them almost anywhere the next day. In addition, its tracking technology contributed significantly to growth. FedEx discovered that customers loved the ability to track their packages because it gave them peace of mind while their packages were in transit and secure confirmation when packages were delivered. Call centers were set up to receive customers' inquiries about the status of their packages. In short order, FedEx had 16 call centers just within the United States.

By 1998, FedEx saw the Internet as a new means of growing its business. It felt that if customers could check on the status of their packaging at any time, day or night, without have to wait on the phone when call centers were busy, customers would have higher satisfaction and give FedEx even more of their business. It would also help FedEx reduce costs by lowering the number of new call center representatives it had to hire and, thereby, help grow earnings. By 1999, the company created a Web site that customers could log into and find a package's status by its unique tracking number.

A somewhat unanticipated consequence of this move occurred when customers phoned into the call centers; they increasingly called with more sophisticated questions in general, along with questions specifically about the Web site. The problem was that call center reps had no access to the Web site and were trained in very narrow specialties. Unable to answer questions about the Web site, they would often pass customers along in a series of call transfers to try to get the various questions answered. Not surprisingly, this often resulted in dropped calls and in delays as the customer waited for the next transfer. Neither result delighted customers. Rather, both often infuriated them.

The challenge of changing the old mental map and moving down a new path to greater growth and profits fell to Laurie Tucker. Her first task was to help senior management see that, with the advent of the Internet, the old call-center approach with specialized reps had now become the wrong thing, and a new vision called *OneCall* must become the right one. To change senior managers' mental maps, Ms. Tucker and her staff created a short video demonstration for the board. It showed a customer calling in while looking at the Web site, posing a number of questions while the call-center rep apologized because he could not see the site. The stunning contrast hit the managers right between the eyes. As a consequence, OneCall was approved. The vision of OneCall was that a customer should be able in one call to get the desired information and not be passed on to someone else.

The target to the employees became clear—answer all customer inquiries to the customer's satisfaction without having to transfer the customer to someone else. Call center reps were initially somewhat anxious about the OneCall vision. Reps had specialized knowledge and wondered how they could possibly answer all questions a customer might ask. This was no idle question because all of them knew from experience that customers were increasingly asking complicated and difficult-to-answer questions. Furthermore, most had little or no experience with the company's Web site. Not only would reps need Web access, they would also need training on how to use the company's Web site and how to walk people through it. In addition, for the OneCall vision to work, call reps would have to be cross-trained in various tasks so that customers would not get passed along in a frustrating series of handoffs. Not one employee was interested in going from being competent to being incompetent. Without all the necessary resources in place, why would they bother trying to walk the OneCall path?

Ms. Tucker and her team made sure that all the necessary resources were provided so the call reps could make the journey. Once call reps had the Web access and training to deliver the OneCall vision, the challenge was getting reps to believe they would be rewarded for walking the new path. Call reps were used to being measured and rewarded on call-time objectives. In other words, the more calls you handled in a day and, therefore, the shorter you made each call, the better. Unfortunately, this contradicted the vision of OneCall. The objective of OneCall was a satisfied customer whose questions were all answered with one call to one rep. As a consequence, the old call-time measures and rewards had to be dropped. Reps were rewarded with bonuses based on customer satisfaction, which included a variety of dimensions, such as efficiency, accuracy, and friendliness. In addition to money, FedEx had supervisors spend more time listening to call rep conversations so that they could praise reps when they solved thorny, time-consuming customer inquiries. As the destination was made clear, the resources put in place, and a mixture of valued rewards presented to reps, they began to believe in and walk the new OneCall path.

The results of achieving this level of belief were significant. In fact, within a few short months, one of the early centers to undergo the transformation generated $10 million in additional sales from delighted customers. With 16 total call centers in the United States alone, similar results at each center could have important financial as well as customer-satisfaction results.

In FedEx's case, whereas the customers and product essentially remained unchanged, growth in revenues and earnings came from changing the how. That change was largely due to the use of new technology. Although the video presentation to top management helped shatter the old map and make way for a new one, that alone was not nearly enough. Unless the call reps were actually able to answer customers' more complicated questions in one call, the new map was no more valuable in growing revenue and earnings than the paper it might have been printed on. The key was getting call reps to believe in the new map and walk the new path.

Achieving

Despite all the time, energy, and money it takes to break through the seeing and moving brain barriers, you still have to break through the failure-to-finish barrier. At the risk of repeating ourselves, this is the barrier that ends up getting the least amount of thought, planning, and priority, and as a consequence, this is the barrier that can crush change initiatives. When this happens, it's like watching a $25 million F-16 hit the sound barrier and crumple like an aluminum can because someone forgot to sweep the wings back. When leaders fail to focus on finishing, all the prior investment to break through the first two barriers is totally wasted.

In many cases, when a change initiative crashes and burns because of a failure to finish, executives fail to recognize the problem as such. They mistakenly think the problem was at the beginning; they conclude that the start was inadequate. As a consequence, they cycle back and start another new change program. They put even more time and energy into fancy slogans and mottos. They roll out training or whatever resources are deemed necessary on an accelerated basis. By this point, employees have grown skeptical of the likely results (not the goodness of the change initiative, per se) and do not put their full faith and support behind the program. Not surprisingly, the extra effort on the front end results only in executives hitting their heads against the failure-to-finish wall sooner. Again, not recognizing the true problem, executives retreat back to the beginning, and a vicious cycle begins and accelerates with each round until the executives are standing alone, banging their heads against the wall while skeptical employees stand off to the side, watching.

Even for companies that do focus on breaking through the failure-to-finish barrier, one of the things they often fail to consider is the spillover impact of their changes on customers and suppliers. As if breaking through the failure-to-finish barrier inside the company weren't hard enough, often the changes you make also require your customers and suppliers to make changes. If customers and suppliers don't also break through the failure-to-finish barrier, they may keep you from achieving the ultimate growth potential of the change initiative.

Dell Computer provides an interesting example of a company that has made significant changes within and has also worked to change its customers and suppliers for growth in revenues and cash flow. In doing so, it did not lose sight of breaking through the failure-to-finish barrier. One of the more interesting and recent examples is its OptiPlex plant.

The PC business has become so price-competitive that gross margins have shrunk to 2%. Consequently, the only way to grow revenue—and especially earnings—is to push costs down and productivity up. With Compaq, Apple, and IBM averaging 50–90 days of finished goods inventory, Dell set the target for its newest plant at *zero*! Yes, zero finished goods inventory. To make good on this objective, the OptiPlex plant has no warehouse. The plant was designed so that finished goods were shipped out of the plant as they came off the assembly line. This was no small task, given that, on average, more than 20,000 machines (PCs, servers, storage boxes, etc.) leave the plant *each day*!

Furthermore, whereas its competitors averaged several weeks of component inventory, Dell set the goal of not two weeks or two days, but two hours of components. To ensure this lean supply system, each of the several receiving docks for different components is roughly 100 square feet, about the size of a large closet. This is also significant when you consider that the plant covers a total of over 200,000 square feet (more than 23 football fields).

Putting in place the automated assembly equipment and software was a significant task, but it has provided impressive benefits. For example, productivity (units produced per person, per hour) increased 160% in just the first year. Although Dell will not reveal the specific return on investment figures for this plant, the company noted that, in 1994, its average return on technological investments was about 30%, whereas in 2000, its ROI was 300%. Clearly impressive. However, without changing the way customers order boxes and changing how suppliers provide components, the automated assembly would grind to a screeching halt. This is the part of the change that is perhaps more interesting and provides a different angle from which we can examine how to overcome the failure to finish.

This new process starts with the customers. Without orders, there are no products to assemble—either by hand labor or by a "lights out" automated factory. In the past, most of Dell's corporate customers had labor-intensive and slow ordering processes. For example, for one customer when employees wanted to order a computer, they had to fill out a requisition form by hand. If they were not careful in reading the hard-to-understand policy guidelines, they would often order a computer with a configuration that was not "approved." Back would come the requisition from the purchasing department to be redone by hand. Even when there was no mistake in the requisition, it would be sent off to the employee's boss, and probably the boss's boss, for approval. When the required approvals were obtained, the requisition would be sent to purchasing. Once there, it would need to be checked to ensure that the requisition specifications met the guidelines; then a purchase order would be issued. Even when the process ran smoothly and there were no mistakes, it took, on average, just over two weeks before a purchase order (PO) was issued. It then took another four weeks for the PO to be processed and a computer finally to show up from Dell. The total time from when the employee put pen (or more sensibly, pencil, with its handy eraser) to paper and a computer's arrival was 36–40 days.

Dell had to help the customer conceive of a better way. Dell's vision had several key components. First, Dell would create a customized catalog for the company. This catalog would consist of products and configurations pre-approved by the company. It would even create pre-approved configurations for different levels in the company. As a consequence, when ordering a computer, an assistant manager could not inadvertently order a computer with features that exceeded the guidelines for that level of position. Once an employee had tapped in his or her order on the custom Web page, a requisition was instantly created and sent electronically to the employee's boss. The boss then had 24 hours to respond, or the request was sent to his or her boss for immediate approval. When approved, a purchase order would be created and sent to Dell. If the requisition was instantly approved when received, the entire process from requisition to when Dell started making the computer could be 60 seconds! With approval of requisitions within 24 hours, instead of the total order to delivery taking 36–40 days, it would now take only 3–4 days.

However, this vision required significant changes for the customer. First, control over the requisition had to be delegated to employees and taken away from central purchasing. Second, bosses had to respond quickly (within 24 hours) or have their bosses know they had not. Third, purchasing departments had to give up playing control cop of PO generation. Fourth, customers had to install software that would link them so tightly to Dell that Dell could see into and begin to recognize patterns in the customers' demand function.

Most customers did not catch the beauty of the vision on their own. They all had entrenched maps, the most significant of which was built on the premise that you never let your supplier see your demand function. The operating premise was "You tell suppliers what you need, not the reverse." To help customers see the need for this change, Dell had to work hard to help customers recognize the cost savings that could come from significantly fewer people handling paper. Dell had to focus on the increased accuracy that also came from fewer manual transcriptions of requisitions to PO to orders to computers. It had to help customers see the productivity benefits of getting employees on their computers in 3 versus 36 days. Ultimately, Dell had to help customers see that these and other benefits were greater than the monetary investments involved and the psychological and political power pain of the change.

However, even when Dell was able to help customers see the need for the change, it still had to help customers believe that the change could be successful. Because most customers had a well-established manual requisition and PO process, the first obstacle to the transition from doing the right thing poorly to doing it well was software. Each customer in most cases had its own proprietary software for keeping track of requisitions, POs, and deliveries. To make matters worse, customers often had different systems for each of these three major functions within their organizations. Dell had to show customers that its software from WebMethods was the resource they needed to integrate effectively. Dell showed customers that because its software was built on open and uniform Internet standards, it could effectively interface with any customer's internal systems.

Even after customers took the plunge and made all the changes, Dell made sure that customers did not get tired or lost and consequently failed to finish. To ensure that customers did not get tired, Dell had dedicated champions assigned to each customer. Especially early on as the customer came on line with the system, it was the champion's job to provide encouragement to customers. One of the key messages to customers was that their efforts were putting them at the cutting edge and, as a consequence, would leave their competitors in the dust. This appeal to pride and sense of competition was quite motivating for customers and kept them fighting through the inevitable glitches and problems of early trials.

Dell also made sure that customers did not feel lost. Dell monitored the results of the change and charted progress. It made sure that the results (good, bad, and ugly) were communicated on a regular basis to customers. Dell reported measures of accuracy, order fulfillment time, and estimated cost savings. As the customer saw the increase in these benefits, sponsors within the customer could continue to fan the flames of motivation and enthusiasm for the change, pushing it to the point where it was well entrenched and clearly successful. For these efforts, customers never got a chance to feel lost and give up. They knew where they were and what progress they were making on a monthly and sometimes weekly basis.

Dell's efforts to get its own suppliers to change and embrace the new vision were equally challenging. Although Dell had more leverage over suppliers to get their buy-in to the vision, the criticality of suppliers effectively and efficiently implementing the change was no less daunting or important.

Suppliers had well-established mental maps that included features such as efficiencies derived from economies of scale in manufacturing and shipping. Suppliers were used to bidding on

and winning large orders from Dell, which they would then produce and ship in large volumes. Furthermore, because these suppliers also had other customers, they had developed internal
processes for allocating product and prioritizing customers when
demand outstripped their internal capacity.

Dell's vision for suppliers was nearly 180 degrees in the opposite
direction of these proven, well-used maps. Dell's vision for suppliers had several key points. First, Dell would download orders
every hour and generate a new manufacturing schedule every
two hours that would reflect changes in job runs and priorities,
as well as components available. Second, suppliers would need to
tie into Dell's system so intimately that suppliers would have
only 15 minutes to confirm an order placed by Dell. Third, once
the order was confirmed, the supplier would then have 75 minutes to get the order to Dell's factory. This meant that suppliers
would have to locate warehouses physically near the Dell factory
that they would supply. Dell's vision required that suppliers keep
two weeks' worth of inventory in these nearby miniwarehouses.

Although Dell was one of the biggest customers, if not the biggest, for many of these suppliers and was the fastest growing PC
manufacturer, many suppliers were reluctant to make the
required changes. Suppliers' mental maps of the past did not
allow customers to see into their capacity, yet the nature of this
integrated system would allow just that. Dell cites the example of
experiencing an up-tick in demand for a specific component,
looking into its supply chain and finding that one supplier had
surplus capacity in one of its offshore factories, then requesting
that the supplier use that capacity to meet the increased
demand. To be clear, Dell did not ask the supplier whether or
how it could meet this up-tick in demand but told the supplier
that it could, as well as where and how.

Although Dell always had the bullet of "dropping" a supplier if
the supplier did not go along with this vision, Dell did not want to

start what would become an intimate relationship with a shotgun marriage proposal. Instead, Dell focused on helping suppliers see the need for the new vision. By tying into the Dell system, suppliers would increasingly have a stable future. It was costly for both parties to become so intimately entwined and, therefore, equally difficult to divorce. By focusing on real-time manufacturing needs, both Dell and suppliers could reduce inventories. Dell's objective was to go from two weeks to two hours of component inventory. Suppliers could, in turn, go from two months to two weeks of finished component inventory for Dell.

Like customers, even if suppliers bought into the vision, they still needed to believe in a path that could help them switch from doing the right thing poorly to doing it well. In the case of suppliers, it was once again software that was the key resource for this path. Dell's software supplier for this part of the vision was i2 Technologies. This software lets suppliers see moment-by-moment demand within Dell for its products and lets Dell see into suppliers' capacity. Dell expected this to increase velocity and save $150 million within the first five years, but it achieved the savings within the first two years.

With such tight tolerances, any hiccup by any supplier can cause serious damage to the overall system. With only a two-hour inventory, most suppliers are delivering several times per day. One missed delivery can shut down the factory.

Consequently, Dell could not afford for a supplier to get tired or lost and, thereby, fail to finish. As with customers, Dell assigned champions to every major supplier at the beginning to encourage them each step of the way. These champions played the role of both technical problem solver and, more importantly, emotional cheerleader. To ensure that suppliers did not get lost, Dell monitored delivery performance constantly. Dell provided both positive and negative feedback about progress. Dell sent out detailed performance reports every month to suppliers to ensure that

starting point for 12 month plan

suppliers knew exactly how they had done, compared with the past, as well as where their performance placed them, relative to other suppliers. If a shipment was late by even a few minutes, Dell generated an instant written (electronic) reprimand. With so much feedback, suppliers had little chance of getting lost.

SUMMARY

Clearly, there is much more involved in the examples we have presented, and in any live cases you encounter, than we could explore in this book. Growth is not the only area of significant strategic change, but it is an important one. This chapter has not attempted to provide a comprehensive discussion of all it takes to grow revenues or profits. Rather, we simply wanted to illustrate that the three barriers and the three principles for breaking through and remapping change can be successfully applied to growth or any other critical challenge.

As we have stressed throughout this book, we are not trying to provide a comprehensive discussion. Both research and practice lead us to believe that, although exhaustiveness can make for long and complete books, it makes for short-lived and unsuccessful practice. People use what they remember. That is why we have focused on the core 20% of change barriers and principles that will get you 80% of the way to your desired result.

9

Leading
Strategic
Change Toolkit:
Conceiving

Collectively, the next four chapters provide the glue to ensure that this all sticks—that it sticks together and that it sticks to you, the reader. After all, if the ideas in *Leading Strategic Change* do not get translated into real actions and success, they offer little lasting value. This transition from the world of principles to the world of practice is critical. The true test of this book's value and your ultimate value to your organization hinges on what you personally put into practice.

When working with literally hundreds of managers over the past decade, we have drawn two conclusions about successfully translating principles into practice. First, most people need a set of useful tools that capture key elements of the principles. Second, leaders add the greatest value to their company by teaching others the principles and helping them put the principles into practice. Great leaders at great companies regularly engage in these high-impact actions. For example, Andy Grove, Chairman of the Board at Intel, was once asked how he found time as a senior executive to train leaders at Intel's supervisory development programs. His instant quip was, "Where can I get more leverage in shaping the future of Intel?" Similarly, Larry Bossidy, CEO of Honeywell and past protégé of Jack Welch at GE, contends, "When you retire, you won't remember what you did in the first quarter of last year, or the third. You'll remember how many people you developed—how many you helped have a better career because of your interest and dedication to their development. When you're confused about how you're doing as a leader, find out how the people you lead are doing. You'll know the answer." For Grove and Bossidy, and any other CEO worth his or her pay, providing the right tools and teaching others how to use them play central roles in leading change.

Building on these two key leadership observations, these next three chapters walk through the complete set of *Leading Strategic Change* principles and provides proven tools that, if used, can help you successfully break through brain barriers in your organization. These tools also provide excellent "teaching and practice aids." In other words, we have found these tools helpful in conveying change principles to others (subordinates, peers, and even superiors) and enhancing their ability to put the principles into practice. The final chapter applies the principles to the most challenging change—anticipatory change.

Although these next three chapters focus on the change toolkit, we all recognize that credibility with others demands that you practice what you preach. Leading by example has endured as one of the most effective leadership principles since time began. If you want others to change, you need to demonstrate your own willingness and ability to change. However, just because you lead does not guarantee that others will follow. This is why we already stated (but it's worth repeating) that the most effective value-adding leaders teach others what they know and how to do it.

INDIVIDUAL CHANGE

We have presented this fundamental principle at the outset of the book, but here it is one last time: Organizational change begins by changing individuals—not the other way around. Even the most ardent believers in organizational change have agreed with us that, at a minimum, organizational change requires some individual "early adopters." Just as in the marketplace, a new product almost never hits immediately. It takes early adopters to get "traction" or momentum. Organizations are the same. If a few individuals in the organization do not adopt the initiative and change their behavior, pulling all the "organizational" levers in the world will produce nothing but sore arms. Like a car, you can change the engine or suspension design but those changes matter only when the rubber hits the road. The changes can look great on paper, but unless the engine redesign gives you greater acceleration or the suspension modification gives you better handling, neither makes a practical difference. Likewise, you can design new corporate strategies, structures, information systems, or shared values, but their impact can materialize only when individuals do something different than before. If changes look great on paper but don't get translated into different behaviors, the changes will not deliver lasting value to shareholders, customers, or employees.

As overwhelming as changing 100,000 or 100 people might seem, in the end, that is what must happen. Consequently, effective change champions must exist throughout the organization. As researchers and consultants, we have rarely seen a ratio greater than one change leader to 100 individuals result in significant, lasting strategic change. This track record emphasizes the need to empower other change champions through example and personal instruction.

By the way, we know that many organizations refer to teaching others using terms or phrases such as *knowledge transfer*. We also know that most everyone but professors hate the notion of "teaching" or "instructing" others. However, whether in a book, article, speech, or consulting engagement, we deliberately use *teach* or *instruct* instead of *knowledge transfer"* or *manage*. We find these less popular words more valuable for change because terms such as *knowledge transfer* often invoke a passive, mechanistic map in people's minds. Transferring knowledge quickly and effectively does not happen by osmosis. To get as many people as possible rapidly capable of strategic change, you must take an active, direct role in teaching them the new principles, as well as coaching them in their application and implementation efforts.

With that introductory framework to this and the other remaining chapters, we now focus on reviewing the principles and discussing the most effective tools around for helping people apply the principles. The three "toolkit" chapters are organized around on our three-part approach to remapping change—CBA (conceiving, believing, achieving).

CONCEIVING TOOLS

If people don't see the need to change, they will not change—unless compelled. Although beating people into submission is possible, it is expensive and results in open rebellions or at the least a quiet return to old habits as soon as the beating stops. Consequently, the most prevalent reason for failed change is the first brain barrier—the failure to see.

INQUISITIVENESS

As discussed in the beginning of this book, we see the need for change only when a contrast is clear. Like a truck far off in the distance, distant opportunities and threats are very hard to see. It is not until the truck blares its horn and nearly smacks into us (or, for some of us, it actually takes getting run over) that we finally notice our well-worn map that had guided us down quiet neighborhood streets is no longer valid. It usually takes this sort of dramatic, "high-impact" event for us to recognize that the world has changed and we are no longer on a quiet country road but, instead, standing in the middle of a busy expressway.

As common as this process is, there are exceptions. Some people consistently see the truck coming long before it blares its horn, but they are rare (at least in our research). Equally rare is that moment when the rest of us actually see the threat or opportunity long before it became incontrovertible. In either case (consistent see-ers and infrequent sight-ers), we found a common factor. These people sought out contrast. They actively questioned their current map. So why, if the current map was working well, did they go out looking for contrast? The common force behind the quest was inquisitiveness.

We say "inquisitiveness" because what we observed in these people was stronger than curiosity and more pragmatic than loving to learn. Inquisitive people and those who experienced a temporary inquisitive spike simultaneously followed their current maps, yet actively questioned their validity. By questioning their mental maps, they purposefully sought out evidence, signs, and signals that contrasted or even contradicted their current maps.

We have found it interesting that without the fuel of inquisitiveness (iQ), actively looking for contrasts such as alternative business models, sales approaches, marketing messages, management styles, or technologies is very exhausting. For low-iQ leaders, searching for new solutions is as attractive as starting a transoceanic flight with only a few gallons of gas in the plane's tank. With only a few gallons in the tank, low-iQ leaders view taking the flight as a significant drain on precious resources, and consequently, they opt to stay on the ground. After all, why fix what isn't broken?

However, high-iQ leaders draw energy from the opportunity to hear new ideas, see new models, visit new markets, etc. They look forward to opportunities to examine issues from new and different perspectives. It gets them up in the morning.

We could go on, but most need little convincing that a high dose of inquisitiveness enhances a person's willingness and ability to change. However, there is a more pragmatic concern. As one manager put it, "Fine, I get it. The more inquisitive your nature, the easier it is for you to recognize and make changes. But can you do anything about the natural level of your inquisitiveness or, for that matter, anyone else's?"

The answer based on research is moderately encouraging. Yes, you can enhance the level of inquisitiveness in you or others, but not infinitely. Research suggests that much of our "natural" inquisitiveness is set by genetics and early childhood experiences (though it seems impossible to disentangle the two and say with precision which, nature or nurture, is more responsible). The questionnaire in Exhibit 9-1 provides a very general sense of your (or others') natural iQ level.

EXHIBIT 9-1   iQ Questionnaire

YOUR IQ INDEX		
1. When confronted with things I don't understand, I am not satisfied until I figure out the answers.	1 2 3 4 5 6	Strongly Disagree Disagree Somewhat Disagree Somewhat Agree Agree Strongly Agree
2. Whenever I need energizing, I find something new to learn about.	1 2 3 4 5 6	Strongly Disagree Disagree Somewhat Disagree Somewhat Agree Agree Strongly Agree
3. Others describe me as a very inquisitive person.	1 2 3 4 5 6	Strongly Disagree Disagree Somewhat Disagree Somewhat Agree Agree Strongly Agree
4. Meeting and getting to know people with unusual backgrounds is interesting and enjoyable.	1 2 3 4 5 6	Strongly Disagree Disagree Somewhat Disagree Somewhat Agree Agree Strongly Agree

EXHIBIT 9-1 iQ Questionnaire *(continued)*

5. Learning new things is more enjoyable than making more money.	1 Strongly Disagree 2 Disagree 3 Somewhat Disagree 4 Somewhat Agree 5 Agree 6 Strongly Agree
6. I frequently enjoy trying new and novel things.	1 Strongly Disagree 2 Disagree 3 Somewhat Disagree 4 Somewhat Agree 5 Agree 6 Strongly Agree
7. I learn something new every day.	1 Strongly Disagree 2 Disagree 3 Somewhat Disagree 4 Somewhat Agree 5 Agree 6 Strongly Agree
8. Compared to most people that I know, I pursue new knowledge in my profession much more actively.	1 Strongly Disagree 2 Disagree 3 Somewhat Disagree 4 Somewhat Agree 5 Agree 6 Strongly Agree
9. People say that I constantly examine experiences and extract the lessons to be learned.	1 Strongly Disagree 2 Disagree 3 Somewhat Disagree 4 Somewhat Agree 5 Agree 6 Strongly Agree
10. I actively seek out unfamiliar places and opportunities to learn when traveling away from home.	1 Strongly Disagree 2 Disagree 3 Somewhat Disagree 4 Somewhat Agree 5 Agree 6 Strongly Agree

Scoring Your iQ Survey. Scoring your survey is relatively simple. Add up the circled numbers for Questions 1–10. The highest possible score is 60. Your total iQ score was _____. Now check to see where your score fits in the following inquisitiveness ratings.

60–50   World-class iQ leaders
49–35   Strong iQ leaders
34–20   Average iQ leaders
19–less Weak iQ leaders

An alternative to the questionnaire above is simply testing yourself or others against the following true story from a high-iQ leader's life and judging what your reaction would be in the same situation. J. Bonner Ritchie reflects world-class inquisitiveness. We have seen it shine in his consulting, teaching, and personal life. For example, several years ago, Bonner was driving with his wife and children on a German autobahn. As he sped down the road, he suddenly realized that he was headed away from his intended destination. Those familiar with the autobahn in Germany know that it can be many kilometers between exits and "on ramps." Rather than wait 15–20 minutes until the next exit, then reenter the highway in the opposite (correct) direction, Bonner considered a shorter route. What looked like a level, grass median separated the lanes of traffic. Bonner thought that if he looked carefully and waited for a break in oncoming traffic, he could cross the grass median and head back in the right direction. Essentially, he was going to make what is commonly called a "U Turn" in the United States. After looking carefully both ways, he pulled onto the left shoulder near a median strip of grass separating the highways. With everything clear, he drove onto the grass to go over to the other side of the highway. Suddenly, the Volvo he was driving rolled over, leaving Bonner and his family suspended upside down in a hidden gully. (The gully was hidden because a long-bladed mowing machine had cut the grass completely level between each side of the freeway.)

Imagine yourself stuck in this situation. There you are, suddenly upside down; you and your family hanging suspended by seat-belts. What are the first words that come out of *your* mouth? When we question executives about this in person, many use expletives that we won't repeat.

As his family dangled, Bonner's first words were not expletives or even inquiries about whether everyone was okay or hurt. Instead, his first words to family members were: "This is interesting. What can we learn from this?" Regardless of your score on the iQ survey in this chapter, if your first instinct in this type of situation is to learn, you top out the inquisitive scale, as Bonner does. *He lives to learn and he learns to live.* His enduring attitude of almost boundless inquiry mirrors what we see over and over in our work with effective change leaders.

The iQ survey and Bonner's high-iQ leadership provide two means for gauging your (or others') level of inquisitiveness, but we must still ask the pragmatic question of how to increase iQ. First, how can you enhance inquisitiveness in yourself? Second, how can you enhance the iQ of others?

Our suggestion for ratcheting up the iQ factor in yourself and others is to reconfigure the whos, wheres, whats, whens, and hows in *your* life. First, consider *your* everyday patterns and the whos in your world. *Who* do you exercise with? *Who* do you ride to work with? *Who* do you take breaks with? *Who* do you eat lunch with? *Who* do you socialize with after work? Now consider your wheres. *Where* do you take walks? *Where* do you eat lunch? *Where* do you vacation? *Where* is the desk in your office? Next, look at the whats. *What* do you read? *What* do you watch? *What* do you hear? *What* do you eat? *What* do you play? *What* do you wear? Don't forget the whens. *When* do you wake up? *When* do you devour pizza? *When* do you drive home from work? *When* do you take long, hot baths? *When* do you reflect? How about your hows? *How* do you brush your teeth? *How* do you fix your breakfast? *How* do you get to work? *How* do you make a sell? *How* do you rejuvenate?

At this point, you might be asking yourself *why* you should care about the whos, wheres, whats, whens, and hows of my life. Put simply, Low-iQ leaders are creatures of habit; high-iQ leaders are masters of innovation. If we want to boost our inquisitiveness, or others' for that matter, we must reconfigure personal routines. During interviews around the world with several hundred high-iQ leaders, we quickly discovered that living without ruts sharpened their inquisitiveness. For example, one high-iQ leader skilled in financial analysis lunched at least once a week with people either outside of the finance group or outside the company (new whos). Another high-iQ leader challenged himself to eating lunch at a different restaurant every day of the week for three straight months—no small feat while living in a city populated by fewer than 300,000 people (new wheres). Frequently, high-iQ leaders learned new skills at work or launched new hobbies at home; others experimented with new foods when traveling in foreign countries; and one executive actually snacked on dried dog food instead of potato chips to win a new client's business in the pet food industry (new whats). Some high-iQ leaders changed their whens by taking Wednesdays off instead of Saturdays or by meeting with customers in the morning instead of the afternoon to catch a glimpse of different work flows. Finally, high-iQ leaders challenged their hows by substituting new approaches to old activities, such as delivering a message in person instead of simply zipping off e-mails.

These examples of new whos, wheres, whats, whens, and hows might seem trivial and at times bizarre, but regularly and consciously upsetting personal routines engages us (and those around us) in everyday learning. And transforming everyday situations into learning opportunities everyday is the fuel for greater inquisitiveness in ourselves and others.

CONTRAST AND CONFRONTATION

Kenneth Chenault, CEO of American Express, recently declared, "The role of a leader is to define reality." We concur. Regardless of whether inquisitiveness is high or low, if *you* recognize the need for change, the real challenge then becomes how to create enough contrast and confrontation so that *others* see the need. As discussed earlier, one key to effective contrast is simplification combined with a focus on the 20/80 principle first discussed in Chapter 1. Although some people can do both in one step, we have found a set of tools for a two-step process more effective with a wider variety of people. The first step is designed to bring into sharper focus what has changed—what the contrasts are. The tool (Exhibit 9-2) is a simple set of questions that uncover common core areas of essential contrast.

Clearly, the questions raised above are not the only relevant ones, but our experience is that if people take the time to answer these questions, it nudges their minds enough out of the trap of current mental maps to begin exploring new alternatives. Once people alter the mental terrain, various contrasts begin to emerge. In fact, typically once the process starts rolling, lots of contrasts become more visible. At this point in remapping change, the objective is to generate as many potential contrasts as possible for each core area listed in the tool (Exhibit 9-2) or other areas you see as important to your business that we have not mentioned.

The next step and task is boiling these contrasts down to the critical few factors—the 20% that paints 80% of the contrast picture. Once you have selected these, you can create a simple matrix (Exhibit 9-3) that will help others clearly see the most important contrasts (just like you did as the CEO of QuadQ, earlier in the book).

EXHIBIT 9-2   Core Areas of Contrast

CORE AREA	KEY QUESTIONS	CRITICAL CONTRASTS
Customers	Are current customer preferences changing?	
	Are our customers' customers changing?	
	Are new customers emerging?	
Competition	Are competitors changing their value proposition to customers?	
	Are competitors gaining or losing specific competitive advantages?	
	Are new competitors emerging?	
Technology	Are current technologies moving ahead of us?	
	Are potential substitute technologies on the horizon?	
	Are new technologies emerging?	
Products and Services	Are current product/service offerings changing?	
	Is the value proposition (price/ offering) ratio changing?	
	Are new products emerging?	

If generating growth is the key driver for change, we can now return to the 3D Growth Cube presented in Chapter 8 as a means of creating a useful tool to highlight and enhance contrasts between past and future growth.

When working with clients, we focus on the shaded cells in the 3D Growth Cube—the areas delivering powerful breakthrough

EXHIBIT 9-3   Critical Factors

CORE AREA	CRITICAL CONTRASTS	
	PAST	FUTURE
Customers		
Competition		
Technology		
Products/Services		

growth (Exhibit 9-4). We do not want to create the impression that there is little opportunity for growth with the existing products, existing customers/markets, and existing approaches cell. Still, our experience causes us to wonder why smart people (including most of your competitors and possibly your firm) continue to try to squeeze the most juice out of this "existing-existing" cell.

As a practical matter, even when we emphasize the shaded cells, we don't ask people to fill in their prime targets for growth directly on the 3D Growth Cube. For many, writing on the cube can be a bit confusing, so we simply break the cube down, using the next set of tools (Exhibit 9-5). These tools are not doing anything wonderful or magical, but they do help us keep our discussion of growth opportunities a bit more organized.

Finally, even if all these tools are utilized and generate insightful contrasts, we warn against stopping here. We have seen, studied, and worked with many leaders who, upon generating what they believed were critical and compelling contrasts, then tried to move forward, only to get knocked back by the unwillingness of others to readily accept the contrasts. Keep in mind Hal's bat-

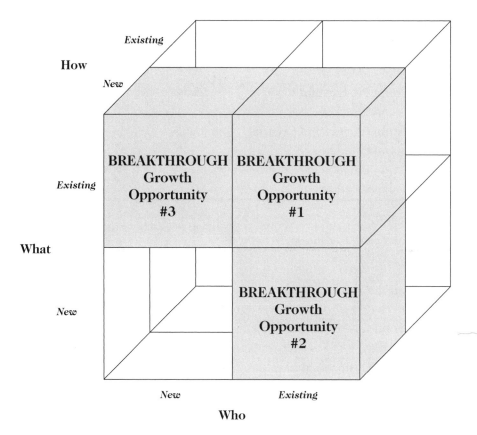

EXHIBIT 9-4
Prime targets for breakthrough growth.

tered and bleeding head when he hit the door jams in Japan again and again. We almost entitled this book "Head-Cracking Change" because of how important inescapable experiences are in changing people's mental maps. But the editor felt that "Head-Cracking Change" might have been a bit too graphic. Still, the point remains. We are all like Hal; it takes more than an intellectual confrontation with the contrast to shake loose deeply entrenched mental maps.

Consequently, you can find a simple tool for breaking through the brain barrier in Exhibit 9-6. We designed it for those leading

EXHIBIT 9-5 Growth Opportunity Tools

EXISTING PRODUCTS AND EXISTING CUSTOMERS/MARKETS	GROWTH OPPORTUNITY #1
	NEW APPROACHES
1. *Existing* Product and *Existing* Customer/Market	Idea 1.
2. *Existing* Product and *Existing* Customer/Market	Idea 2.
3. *Existing* Product and *Existing* Customer/Market	Idea 3.
4. *Existing* Product and *Existing* Customer/Market	Idea 4.

EXISTING CUSTOMERS/ MARKETS	GROWTH OPPORTUNITY #2	
	NEW PRODUCTS	NEW APPROACHES
1. *Existing* Customer/Market	Idea 1.	
2. *Existing* Customer/Market	Idea 2.	
3. *Existing* Customer/Market	Idea 3.	
4. *Existing* Customer/Market	Idea 4.	

EXISTING PRODUCTS	GROWTH OPPORTUNITY #3	
	NEW CUSTOMERS/ MARKETS	NEW APPROACHES
1. *Existing* Products	Idea 1.	
2. *Existing* Products	Idea 2.	
3. *Existing* Products	Idea 3.	
4. *Existing* Products	Idea 4.	

EXHIBIT 9-6   Tool for *Breaking through the Brain Barrier*

CORE AREA	POTENTIALLY HIGH-CONFRONTATION EXPERIENCES (SENSORY ENGAGEMENT: SIGHT, SOUND, SMELL, TASTE, TOUCH)
Customers	
Competition	
Technology	
Products/Services	

the change. Its objective is to help you construct inescapable experiences for each critical contrast that you have worked so hard to identify. Again, from experience, it seems most effective to examine potential confrontations by category. In other words, we ask people to generate ideas on how to inescapably confront each area of contrast.

You can gain two primary benefits from taking this sequential approach to creating contrasts. First, even when you do a good job zeroing in on critical contrasts, you can often end up with too many to tackle all at once. Second, by examining potential confrontations in sequence, we find it easier to spot possible combinations.

For example, if we return to QuadQ, you may remember the idea of bringing in one of the new end users (a technician with an associates degree—not a PhD, sporting purple hair—not a lab coat) to try out QuadQ's old technology. Compared with old end users of your products, this new technician's obvious fumbling with your *un*friendly user interface creates an inescapable experience that highlights critical contrasts relative to *both* customers and technology.

From our experience, trying to identify from the outset high-impact "two-for-one" or "three-for-one" experiences where you can confront two or more critical contrasts through one experience is very hard to do. Although it may seem somewhat tedious, you should find greater success if you explore potential high-confrontation experiences in sequence, rather than all at once.

After working through the tools for identifying and highlighting critical contrasts and generating high-confrontation experiences, you are in a great position to help people really see the need for change in your organization. Once they see the need (or alternatively, conceive a new map), you have thrust—the power to take off—but still need the next key, lift, for people to actually believe they can travel to the new destination.

10

LEADING STRATEGIC CHANGE TOOLKIT: BELIEVING

P eople must conceive the need for change, but this alone is not sufficient. Simply recognizing that the old right thing is now wrong is not enough. They must clearly envision the new right thing *and* believe in a path that will take them from doing the new right thing poorly to doing it well. Once they believe in the path, you can get the lift needed to overcome their failure to move. As discussed earlier, the three keys to lift and movement are destinations, resources, and rewards. Next we want to review these principles briefly and highlight some practical tools for ensuring movement.

DESTINATIONS

People not only need to recognize that the old thing is now wrong, but they must also see with clarity what the new right thing is. Although this is a necessary step, it alone cannot deliver movement to change. People also need to envision where they are headed as they move forward; they must see the new promised land in their mind's eye. It's one thing to say, "In the past, we practiced customer indifference, but in the future, we will put customers first." It is quite another to translate the promised land of Customer 1st into clear targets that individuals can aim at and actually hit.

This is why the key practical step in establishing effective targets is translating the vision of the new right thing into concrete behaviors. For example, if Customer 1st is the new vision, what will that look like in terms of behavior? How would you recognize Customer 1st behavior if you saw it? For example, in the case of Sam, our airline gate agent, when a customer comes late to the gate, one concrete behavior of the new Customer 1st vision is empathizing with customer frustration at missing flights. Another behavior is proactively working to help customers get to their destinations. Only when targets are this concrete and clear will Sam move forward.

A consistent exercise we engage managers in is clarifying the new right thing in terms of concrete behaviors. The more complex the vision in which the new right thing must be accomplished, the greater the need first to define the most common situations that will create that complex change, then to describe the concrete behaviors in those situations that support the new vision. For example, in Sam's case, one of the most common situations for making the vision of Customer 1st a reality happens when someone arrives late to the gate. Another common situation occurs when flights are delayed or cancelled. The tool in Exhibit 10-1 can help you define key situations in your change initiative, then describe in detail the relevant desired behaviors.

This approach to change may seem detailed, but we have noticed two important implications in our research and work with clients. First, without clear and concrete target behaviors, most people will not move. So, although it may take a bit of time and effort to detail the most common situations and describe the targeted behaviors, the negative returns for not doing this, compared with the positive returns for the time and effort for doing it, make the decision to invest an easy one. Second, we have discovered that if you focus on the 20% of situations—and related target behaviors—that cover 80% of the new vision, the rest of the less core situations and behaviors take care of themselves.

What do we mean that the rest take care of themselves? To illustrate, return to Sam our airline gate agent. For Sam, two situations—customers arriving late and delayed (or cancelled) flights—are within the critical core 20% that account for 80% of all customer service situations. By knowing what the targeted behaviors are for these core situations, Sam can "fill in the blanks" regarding Customer 1st behaviors for less common situations reasonably well on his own. That is, as Sam encounters the

EXHIBIT 10-1   Identifying Situations and Desired Response Behaviors

COMMON SITUATION	TARGETED BEHAVIOR
A.	1.
	2.
	3.
B.	1.
	2.
	3.
C.	1.
	2.
	3.
D.	1.
	2.
	3.

other less common situations, he can reasonably extrapolate from the identified core situations and make reasonably sound judgments as to what the targeted behaviors should be. The implication of this point is critical. If you take the time and invest the resources to identify the core 20% of situations and describe the related target behaviors, you will not need to make the same resource investment in the remaining; you will have equipped your people to do that job for you.

RESOURCES

Now your people should have a clear idea of the target. Part of their "motivation to move" equation is solved. Next, you must ensure that they believe they have the resources to make the journey. Remember, we are talking about a wide variety of resources—tools, knowledge, capabilities, etc.—to make change happen. Movement requires that movers believe they have what it takes. For example, people can have the sales capabilities but lack product knowledge and, as a consequence, lack the motivation to move.

To support movement fully, we use the charts in Exhibit 10-2 to help map out the full spectrum of required resources. These charts also help you identify the necessary actions to supply your people with needed resources so that they can individually bridge the gap between what they have and what they need.

EXHIBIT 10-2   Required Resources Charts

CAPABILITIES			
OLD	NEW	GAP	BRIDGE
		Small	1.
		Medium	
			2.
		Large	
		Small	1.
		Medium	
			2.
		Large	
		Small	1.
		Medium	
			2.
		Large	
		Small	1.
		Medium	
			2.
		Large	
		Small	1.
		Medium	
			2.
		Large	
		Small	1.
		Medium	
			2.
		Large	

EXHIBIT 10-2   Required Resources Charts *(continued)*

KNOWLEDGE			
OLD	NEW	GAP	BRIDGE
		Small	1.
		Medium	
		Large	2.
		Small	1.
		Medium	
		Large	2.
		Small	1.
		Medium	
		Large	2.
		Small	1.
		Medium	
		Large	2.
		Small	1.
		Medium	
		Large	2.
		Small	1.
		Medium	
		Large	2.

EXHIBIT 10-2   Required Resources Charts *(continued)*

OTHER RESOURCES			
OLD	NEW	GAP	BRIDGE
		Small	1.
		Medium	
			2.
		Large	
		Small	1.
		Medium	
			2.
		Large	
		Small	1.
		Medium	
			2.
		Large	
		Small	1.
		Medium	
			2.
		Large	
		Small	1.
		Medium	
			2.
		Large	
		Small	1.
		Medium	
			2.
		Large	

REWARDS

Once people can see the targets clearly and believe they have what it takes to hit the targets, the remaining key to movement is instilling a belief that they will receive valued rewards along the path to the desired change. As discussed before, most managers need little help in using financial incentives to motivate movement. However, financial incentives are expensive, and they are not always completely within the control of those trying to lead the change. In addition, many other, more readily available rewards are just as powerful and often more motivating than traditional financial incentives.

Here we want to reiterate that, although everyone is likely motivated to some extent by all of the following, they are not motivated equally. This is why it is worth the time and effort to consider key people who need to move or change and generate a clear image of their most powerful motivators, as well as what actions you can take to produce those motivators.

We use the tool in Exhibit 10-3 to help with this diagnosing and planning process. We start by identifying the key individuals to motivate and move. In every organization or subunit, we always find key informal leaders and trend-setters. Quite often, if you can get them moving, others follow. Next, we go through each of the motivation areas and sub-areas on the chart to determine which we believe to be the top three most powerful in motivating that specific individual. Finally, for each of the top three areas, we write out a few concrete actions that can be taken to motivate the person. Again, although this tool represents a significant investment of time and energy, the negative consequences of not performing this step and the positive payoffs of spending the time and effort make it one you can't afford to skip.

EXHIBIT 10-3   Tool for Determining Motivation of Key Individuals

KEY INDIVIDUAL:			
AREA	**SUB-AREA**	**TOP 3**	**ACTION**
Achievement	Accomplishment	Yes	1.
		No	2.
	Competition	Yes	1.
		No	2.
Relations	Approval	Yes	1.
		No	2.
	Belonging	Yes	1.
		No	2.
Conceptual/	Problem Solving	Yes	1.
Thinking		No	2.
	Coordination	Yes	1.
		No	2.
Improvement	Growth	Yes	1.
		No	2.
	Exploration	Yes	1.
		No	2.
Control	Competence	Yes	1.
		No	2.
	Influence	Yes	1.
		No	2.

Summary

With clear destinations, required resources, and valued rewards, you can break through the failure-to-move barrier. With that breakthrough, you now must work to sustain the change and achieve lasting results. Overcoming the final barrier to change—failure to finish—may well be the most difficult.

11

LEADING STRATEGIC CHANGE TOOLKIT: ACHIEVING

In many ways, failing to finish represents the saddest of the three failures. It is disheartening to see so much time and energy (to say nothing of money) funneled into a strategic change, only to watch it go down the drain as people get tired and become lost.

CHAMPIONS

People get tired primarily by doing the right thing poorly at first. Virtually no one, and certainly not large groups of people, become instantly proficient at following new maps, especially if they are radically different from the past. Even when people are motivated to try, they make mistakes. These mistakes or performances at less than ideal levels of proficiency generate negative consequences. People get worn out as they try to do the right thing but fail to obtain the desired results.

This is why change champions are needed where the rubber meets the road. Champions reinforce the desired behaviors, even when the right efforts do not generate the desired results—at first. To ensure that champions are in place to compensate for this initial gravitational inertia, we provide two straightforward tools.

The first tool (Exhibit 11-1) helps you make explicit three key elements of championing:

1. **Rubber-meets-the-road behaviors.** It is absolutely critical to identify in advance the "rubber-meets-the-road" behaviors necessary for the strategic change. What must be different for the change to gain traction and produce an impact?

2. **Likely negative consequences of initial poor proficiency.** It is helpful to identify in advance likely negative consequences for less than ideal proficiency in following the new map. At a minimum, champions need a clear idea of what

these consequences will be. We have found that making them explicit and explaining them to those making the change is also helpful. This way, when people obtain undesired consequences while trying to do the right thing, they will not become as tired or discouraged.

3. **Key champion actions.** Finally, it is important to make explicit what actions change champions should take when people exhibit the right behaviors but do not get the desired consequences. Without taking this third step, you simply leave to chance—a roll of the dice—that change champions will take the appropriate steps to compensate for the downward drag or even change-breaking effects that early negative consequences can generate.

We use the chart in Exhibit 11-1 to help change champions map out these three key elements.

EXHIBIT 11-1 Key Elements of Championing Change

RUBBER MEETS THE ROAD BEHAVIORS	LIKELY NEGATIVE CONSEQUENCES OF INITIAL POOR PROFICIENCY	KEY CHAMPION ACTIONS
1.	1.	1.
	2.	2.
1.	1.	1.
	2.	2.
1.	1.	1.
	2.	2.
1.	1.	1.
	2.	2.
1.	1.	1.
	2.	2.
1.	1.	1.
	2.	2.

Stopping here, however, assumes that champions capably provide the needed compensatory actions to balance negative consequences. From our experience, this is not always the case. Just as the new map is likely to require individuals to engage in new behaviors, it is also likely to require new behaviors of change champions in breaking through this segment of the failure-to-finish barrier. Therefore, simply but systematically assessing required capabilities, current capabilities, resulting gaps, and needed bridging actions is a must for breakthrough change. The chart in Exhibit 11-2 will help you do this assessment.

EXHIBIT 11-2   Change Champion Assessment Tool

CHAMPION ASSESSMENT			
REQUIRED CAPABILITY	CURRENT CAPABILITY	GAP	BRIDGING ACTIONS
		Yes	1.
		No	2.
		Yes	1.
		No	2.
		Yes	1.
		No	2.
		Yes	1.
		No	2.
		Yes	1.
		No	2.
		Yes	1.
		No	2.
		Yes	1.
		No	2.
		Yes	1.
		No	2.

Using these two tools, you will gain a clear understanding of where and why people will likely get tired, and you will have the champions and actions in place to compensate for the sluggishness. These tools will help you maintain change momentum until improvements in proficiency can produce positive consequences that naturally reinforce desired behaviors.

CHARTING

Unfortunately, even if champions are placed well and reward the desired behaviors to compensate for the early negative consequences to change, people can still become lost. They can lose track of where they are, how much progress they have (or haven't) made, and how the change is going for others. To keep people from feeling lost and giving up, charting and communicating progress play a pivotal role. As already discussed, these actions must be done at both individual and group levels. The appropriate group level may be a work group or an entire company. That decision depends largely on the nature of the change. The larger the change and the more dramatic the strategic shift for the company, the more information must be gathered at various levels, including the company level, and communicated back to people.

Except for the simplest of change initiatives, there are typically dozens of measures of progress that we might look at, creating hundreds of messages that then must be communicated to people. To describe this challenge, we take examples from flying and driving. Although confronted with potentially hundreds of cues, effective pilots and drivers alike focus on a few instruments that measure key elements. Consequently, these instruments are usually easily seen in a "heads-up" display on a plane or in the dashboard on a car. In airplanes, speed, altitude, and heading are

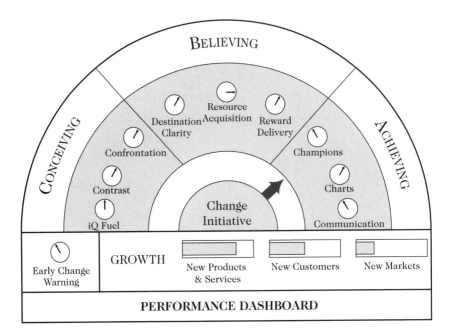

EXHIBIT 11-3
Leading strategic change performance dashboard.

key elements to measure. Likewise, any change initiative must include a *limited* number of key elements to monitor. You might think of this as your heads-up display or "performance dashboard" for change measurement, as shown in Exhibit 11-3.

There are five preparation steps to creating and monitoring your performance dashboard:

1. **Element to measure.** First, you should identify what you believe to be the key elements to measure (for example, attitudes and/or actions). If we return to our gate agent, Sam, customer complaints are clearly an important measure of whether the Customer 1st initiative is working. Customer satisfaction may also be an important element to measure.

2. **Method of Measurement.** It is also helps to establish how the key element will be measured. For example, an airline

might measure complaints based on the number of written complaints received per 1,000 passengers. Customer satisfaction might be measured via a survey given to a random set of customers.

3. **Measurement Interval.** It's important to establish how often the measures will be taken. Some measures are more difficult and costly to procure than others, and other outcomes take longer to formulate. Therefore, measures are useful only if taken with longer time intervals between assessments.

4. **Baseline Measurement.** Once key elements and methods of measurement are determined, establishing a baseline of performance is critical before the change initiative gets underway. Without a baseline, it is difficult to determine how much progress is being made.

5. **Target Results.** Finally, establishing target performance levels is also critical. Should Sam be shooting for less than 10 complaints per month or less than one? The chart in Exhibit 11-4 can help you to capture these change measurement issues.

EXHIBIT 11-4   Change Measurement Chart

ELEMENT TO MEASURE	METHOD OF MEAS'MT.	MEAS'MT. INTERVAL	BASELINE MEAS'MT.	TARGET RESULTS

When it comes to charting progress on these measures, there are as many approaches as there are companies. As far as we know, no research says definitively that one method of charting progress is more effective than any other. We can say from our experience that graphs have a stronger impact on people than the mere numbers behind them and that charts showing progress over time, relative to the final destination, help people the most to avoid feeling lost. Exhibit 11-5 presents a sample chart to illustrate these two points.

With the key elements of measure established, your next step is determining the general communication plan. Entire books are devoted to effective communication plans, so we won't try to reproduce all those ideas here. Rather, we will stick to the fundamentals that everyone knows but that are useful to review.

Any communication plan starts by determining *who* the information receiver will be. In our experience, companies tend to

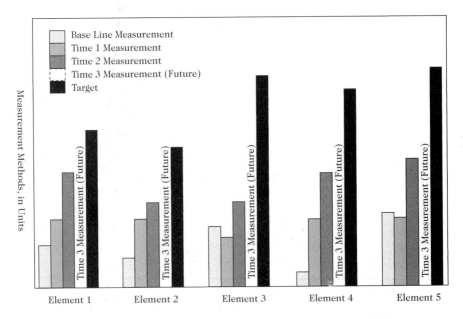

EXHIBIT 11-5
Chart of change progress.

error in the direction of sharing change progress with too few people. Whenever we assess employees' satisfaction with communication, especially related to strategic change initiatives, we have never found a situation where employees felt that too many people were informed as to how things were progressing. In almost every case, employees who were excluded from the communication believed that they should have been included. We are not suggesting that these employees were always right and should have been included, but their feelings do illustrate how much easier it is to error on the side of limiting the "who" of communication plans too much than in expanding the recipient list too far.

Next, the communication plan should determine *what* will be shared. As mentioned earlier in the book, it's best to share the good, the bad, and even the ugly. To think that certain people can help you bring about a needed change and to believe that they are not mature enough to understand how the change is really going communicates a double standard, loudly and clearly.

When is the third element to determine in a communication plan. As already mentioned, we should take some measurements more often than others. Consequently, in some cases, not everything is communicated at the same time. In general, it's a mistake to wait until everything is available before communicating anything. People can easily feel lost while waiting for perfect information; therefore, some information sooner is better than all the information later.

Finally, in this age of various communication mediums, deciding on *how* to communicate progress presents unique challenges. Due to the range of options (e-mail, voice mail, "snail mail," video, face to face, presentations, etc.), you may need to choose a different medium for different times or for different content. For example, content such as declining customer satisfaction scores after the launch of a Customer 1st program is probably

EXHIBIT 11-6   Exhibit 11.6 Change Communication Plan

COMMUNICATION PLAN			
WHO	WHAT	WHEN	HOW

best communicated through more complex and rich mediums, such as live presentations or videos, versus mass e-mails. Again, this book's purpose is not to outline all the details and nuances to designing a communication plan but simply to reinforce that a plan is necessary and that you should incorporate who, what, when, and how into it. The chart in Exhibit 11-6 provides a place to map out the basics of your change communication plan.

SUMMARY

With the right champions in the right place—where the rubber meets the road—and with the right heads-up display of core measures, combined with a plan to communicate them, you have created the key elements to break through the final brain barrier—failure to finish. After breaking through the barriers of failure to see, failure to move, and failure to finish, then firmly establishing a new map for the new destination, the only problem remaining for remapping change is guarding against our natural tendency to become trapped once again by the new map that we have so faithfully followed.

12

GETTING AHEAD OF THE CHANGE CURVE

Having touched on the final challenge of the timing of change, let's conclude with a direct assault on the issue. We are compelled to do this because the payoff to you and your company can be significant. Three tactics to timing change—anticipatory, reactive, and crisis—frame our options for the future.

Anticipatory change is just that—anticipating the need for change. In other words, anticipatory change demands that we look ahead to see in advance the signs that show change on the horizon. This approach helps us to recognize early that the old right map may soon become wrong. Then, based on this recognition, the challenge we face is trying to figure out in advance what the new right map should be.

Reactive change is equally well titled. This approach revolves around reacting to obvious signs and signals that change is needed. These signs and signals surface from customers, competitors, shareholders, employees, and other critical stakeholders, indicating that we should change today or likely pay a heavier price tomorrow.

Crisis change confronts a company when the signs and signals have multiplied and intensified to the point of undeniability—undeniable because, at this point, our competitors have already begun to change, and we're still sitting on the sidelines. When signs and signals have been ignored too long, you can count on the consequences showing up a firm's financial performance. No doubt you can remember dozens of companies that have faced crisis change. For example, Nissan ignored the signals for so long that a foreigner, Carlos Gohen, was brought in to manage the crisis. With Kmart, the crisis has escalated so far that history is in the making as Kmart competes for the biggest retail bankruptcy record in U.S. history. At this point, it is not clear how many crisis or turnaround change agents Kmart will need before returning to its former glory—if it ever will.

We have found these three approaches to change quite useful because they are intuitively straightforward. There is nothing hard to understand about the essential elements to each of them. Yet some subtle, counter-intuitive issues still exist underneath each approach. Let's examine each in more detail.

Fundamentally, the more you drift down the slope from anticipatory change to crisis change, the easier it is to get the change going. For obvious reasons, to initiate anticipatory change when the signs and signals indicating its need are far off in the distance is the most difficult. As Andy Grove, Chairman of the Board at Intel, recently confessed, "Half of our employees have only seen record earnings, quarter after quarter. There's a feeling of invulnerability, which is death."

Once the signs and signals of change start showing up at your door with frequency, they are harder to deny. Consequently, reactive change is easier to get going than is anticipatory change. The signs and signals may become so vast, severe, and incessant that they become undeniable. Kicking off crisis change is the easiest because the patient is almost ready to keel over, lying sick and bleeding on the battlefield. These increasing difficulties to initiating change are shown in Exhibit 12-1.

However, as we slide down the slippery slope of the change curve from anticipation to crisis, the costs of change also grow (Exhibit 12-2). Anticipatory change is hard, but the costs are significantly less in the long run, compared with cutting out half of the work force, idling expensive plants, and damaging the reputation of the firm in the eyes of customers, suppliers, and society.

If you were to superimpose Exhibit 12-1 on Exhibit 12-2, you could see that the difficulty and costs of change along these three approaches to change—anticipatory, reactive, and crisis—are inversely related to each other. As difficulty of change increases, costs of change decline. Conversely, as costs increase, difficulty declines. To see why this is the case, let's dig below the surface on this powerful dynamic by starting with the last approach first—crisis change.

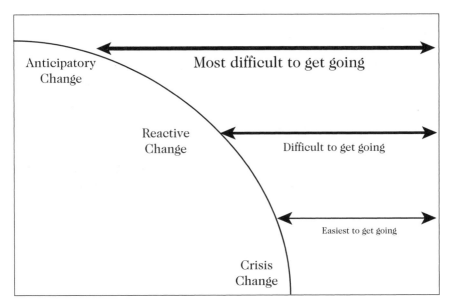

EXHIBIT 12-1
The difficulty of change.

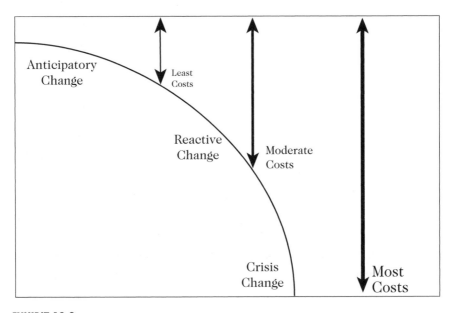

EXHIBIT 12-2
The costs of change.

CRISIS CHANGE

Most people we work with usually think crisis change is the hardest of the three. After all, in the worst scenarios, company survival is on the line. For example, we already outlined the crisis Xerox faced when it brought in Rick Thoman from IBM, who by all accounts was quite capable and successful in the past. Yet Thoman lasted less than two years at the helm. Facing an even deeper crisis and continued losses in the tens of millions of dollars, Xerox brought in another new CEO to try to turn things around.

How would you like to be the new CEO? Tough job, right? Yes and no. Clearly, turning a company around is never simple, but in terms of getting change going, crisis change is the easiest of the three to lead. After all, when your credit ratings are downgraded monthly, when losses mount daily, and when your stock price falls hourly, how hard is it to convince people that the old map is now wrong? Also, how precise do the dramatic measures that must be taken need to be? For example, if labor costs are excessive, how hard is it to cut a third of your work force? How much precision does that really take? It may require a strong stomach, but how not much skill is required to initiate the change?

As an analogy for this corporate situation, compare the worlds of a battlefield medic and vascular surgeon. How much training does a battlefield medic need, compared with a vascular surgeon? A battlefield medic's training is measured in months, whereas a vascular surgeon's is measured in years. Why? Imagine yourself on a battlefield where someone's arm is shattered by an explosion. Bullets are whizzing overhead. The enemy is advancing. What do you do? You are clearly in a crisis. You can't take time to try to patch the arm back together carefully. No, you put a tourniquet on the arm to stop the bleeding, and now! Perhaps the soldier loses the arm. Maybe you have to cut off the arm to save the person. If you do, there isn't time for precision; you're in a crisis. Maybe you should have cut it off an inch higher or lower than you did, but there's no time to worry about that. Indeed, if you had the time and were not in a crisis, as a vascular surgeon, you could perform the seven-hour operation to restore the torn muscles and reconnect the severed blood vessels.

Please don't misunderstand us. We are not suggesting that anyone can become a battlefield medic or that anyone can perform a successful company turnaround. However, we are saying that the inherent nature of crisis change makes it much easier to break through the failure-to-see barrier, as well as the failure-to-move barrier, in comparison with anticipatory change. After all, if you don't see or move when a crisis hits, you are as good as dead.

However, just as the battlefield crisis results in more blood, suffering, and loss of life or limb, so, too, does crisis change. Crisis change almost always costs money, shareholder value, customer loyalty, and jobs—the livelihoods for often large numbers of employees. Thus, although crisis change is the easiest of the three to initiate, it is also the most costly for almost everyone affected by it.

REACTIVE CHANGE

Reactive change is probably the most common approach we see in organizations. Reactive change is harder to get going than crisis change because less evidence exists that the successful map of the past is indeed wrong for the future. It is typically less costly than crisis change because it usually happens before the red ink flows freely and before the work force must be cut in half for sheer survival. Take notice, though, we do not want to create the impression that reactive change is bad, per se. The more uncertain the signs and signals that the business environment is shifting, the more prudent it may be to wait and react. In fact, if you have established a general level of change agility within your organization, it may be much better to respond as a quick second mover instead of a first mover. However, the junk pile of derailed careers of leaders who were slow second movers is both high and wide. While an ever-present great temptation looms for firms to drift down the slippery slope from anticipatory to reactive change, you must remember and count the very real costs and consequences of failing to pull off anticipatory change.

ANTICIPATORY CHANGE

Everyone knows from experience that anticipatory change is very hard—initially. Just as it is difficult to see physical objects when they are far off in the distance, so, too, is it hard to help people sense business threats or opportunities when they are either on or sometimes over the sight horizon. Furthermore, even if we do help others to see these distant threats or opportunities, the farther away they are, the greater is the chance that they can change course, and as a result, we will miss them as time and distance slip by. We all know that being off by even a small degree over a long time and great distance can easily lead to missing a target by a wide margin. In fact, the longer the time and distance we travel, the greater will be the magnitude of the miss when off by only a degree or two at the start.

We all understand this dynamic, so most of us are nervous about the time, energy, money, and other valuable investments required for successful anticipatory change. With anticipatory change, many feel a greater chance of missing the future target and getting no good return on current investments. This tendency is strongly reinforced if the current map that we follow not only works well now but has worked well for quite some time.

This is no doubt a big reason why many executives avoid antici-patory change. Of the three types of change, it is the most diffi-cult to start and, as a result, the most difficult to finish.

Anticipatory change also presents the greatest potential benefits and lowest costs to the firm—if executed correctly. *You* can also accrue significant career benefits by mastering anticipatory change. Because anticipatory change is difficult, the supply of capable anticipatory change leaders is short. Career premiums are always paid when demand outstrips supply. Because a short-age of anticipatory change leaders continues, first-mover advan-tages are real for organizations, and the potentially payoffs are enormous.

This is especially true when the change involves long and steep learning curves. You might be inclined to conclude just the oppo-site. After all, long and steep learning curves (reflecting the sig-nificant amount of learning required to do the new right thing well) mean that the payoffs do not show up initially. However, it is for precisely that reason that the sooner you get your com-pany on the curve, the greater will be your firm's advantage over slower-to-change competitors. As Exhibit 12-3 and Exhibit 12-4 illustrate, for each equal interval of time during the learning pro-cess, once you get into the "fat" part of the learning curve, the greater becomes your advantage and the distance you put between yourself and your competitors.

For example, consider the rivalry between Pepsi and Coke in Vietnam (with its 80 million people). The learning curves for manufacturing, distributing, and selling beverages in Vietnam are long and steep. Understanding and mastering the nuances of working effectively with a joint venture partner that was a former state-owned enterprise alone are vast. Workers must be hired and trained to focus not just on volume, but also on qual-ity. Because the nature of the market is quite fractured, literally dozens and dozens of relationships with distributors have to be

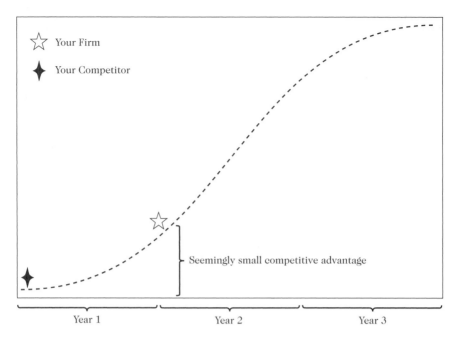

EXHIBIT 12-3
Moving fast and first up steep learning curves: Year 1.

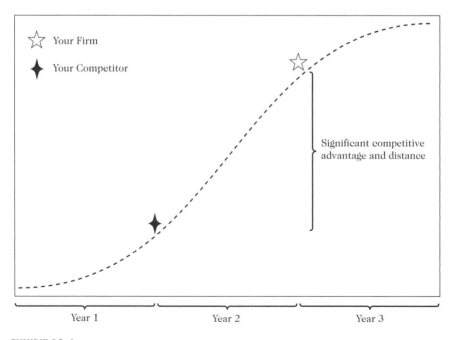

EXHIBIT 12-4
Moving fast and first up steep learning curves: Year 2.

formed in order to get your product to the market. The retail shops for distribution to the consumer market are so fragmented that it takes literally thousands of relationships with "mom-and-pop" shops just to get your product out in the south of Vietnam. Now add to this challenge the learning curves of marketing and advertising Pepsi products. What it takes to sell your product in the United States will not necessarily get you the results you want in Vietnam. Hundreds of differences and pitfalls are lurking out there. For example, you must be careful that your slogan, "Come alive with the new Pepsi generation," does not get translated mistakenly as "Pepsi will bring your ancestors back from the dead," which actually happened in one of its ads that was translated into Chinese.

Finally, do all the investments of anticipatory change associated with going for growth in emerging markets deliver company results immediately? No. Coke followed Pepsi into Vietnam only a year or two later, and the distance between them initially seemed small. However, when Pepsi entered into the fat part of the learning curve, the benefits of its anticipatory change became more evident. Today, Pepsi rules the economically vibrant southern part of Vietnam. Coke is taking refuge in the north. Who will ultimately win this competition? It is hard to say, but Pepsi made the early anticipatory moves and continues to enjoy the lead.

FINAL THOUGHTS

Let's finish *Leading Strategic Change* with a few final thoughts. First, even though we spent a good part of this chapter discussing anticipatory change, it is not the only approach to change. Furthermore, none of us spends all of our time in the world of anticipatory change. We may well slip unintentionally into reactive change or find ourselves thrust into a change crisis. To make sure that there is no misunderstanding, the principles of *Leading Strategic Change* work as well in reactive and crisis change settings as they do for anticipatory change.

However, we concluded this final chapter with a discussion of anticipatory change for a specific reason. Because anticipatory change is the most difficult, that is where the supply of successful change leaders is the smallest. Also, because anticipatory change is where the potential payoffs are the biggest, that is where demand for successful change leaders is the greatest. From our extensive consulting work and research, the conclusion is clear. Anticipatory change leaders are in great demand and extremely short supply.

Demand outstripping supply is the most powerful reason for mastering the art and science of remapping change. In this book, we have shared some powerful principles of change that can help you break through the brain barriers of failure to see, failure to move, and failure to finish. In the previous three chapters, we have supplied you with concrete, practical tools to become a master mapmaker at work. The key to breaking through the brain barriers to change lie not just in grasping the principles, but also in applying them in practice.

To put these principles into practice, they must become personal. To help illustrate this, consider the following. Hal's father was one of those old-time dads who could fix anything. To do this, he studied the principles of electricity, mechanics, fluids, and construction. When it came time to fix a diesel engine, gasoline engine, or refrigerator motor, he was a master at putting the principles into practice. His shop was full of almost every tool you could imagine—and some you couldn't. The ones you couldn't imagine were those he created himself. Because he understood what needed to be fixed and how to fix it well, when the right tool wasn't commercially available, he made it. Similarly to Hal's father, we hope not only that you can master these principles and practices for breaking through the change barriers, but also that you can create unique tools for the specific demands faced in your change initiatives.

To finish our journey, then, let's go back to the beginning. Strategic change starts from the inside out. We change individuals by remapping minds so they can conceive, believe, and achieve a new destination. By changing individuals, we change organizations. That's our core conviction, reflected in the *Leading Strategic Change* principles. As a leader in today's highly unpredictable business terrain, you now have the tools to become an even more accomplished mental cartographer—a Master Map Maker in a world full of change.

INDEX

8 reasons why you should read the Financial Times for 4 weeks RISK-FREE!

To help you stay current with significant developments in the world economy ...
and to assist you to make informed business decisions — the Financial Times brings you:

1 Fast, meaningful overviews of international affairs ... plus daily briefings on major world news.

2 Perceptive coverage of economic, business, financial and political developments with special focus on emerging markets.

3 More international business news than any other publication.

4 Sophisticated financial analysis and commentary on world market activity plus stock quotes from over 30 countries.

5 Reports on international companies and a section on global investing.

6 Specialized pages on management, marketing, advertising and technological innovations from all parts of the world.

7 Highly valued single-topic special reports (over 200 annually) on countries, industries, investment opportunities, technology and more.

8 The Saturday Weekend FT section — a globetrotter's guide to leisure-time activities around the world: the arts, fine dining, travel, sports and more.

FT FINANCIAL TIMES
World business newspaper

The *Financial Times* delivers a world of business news.

Use the Risk-Free Trial Voucher below!

To stay ahead in today's business world you need to be well-informed on a daily basis. And not just on the national level. You need a news source that closely monitors the entire world of business, and then delivers it in a concise, quick-read format.

With the *Financial Times* you get the major stories from every region of the world. Reports found nowhere else. You get business, management, politics, economics, technology and more.

Now you can try the *Financial Times* for 4 weeks, absolutely risk free. And better yet, if you wish to continue receiving the *Financial Times* you'll get great savings off the regular subscription rate. Just use the voucher below.

---

4 Week Risk-Free Trial Voucher

Yes! Please send me the *Financial Times* for 4 weeks (Monday through Saturday) Risk-Free, and details of special subscription rates in my country.

Name_____

Company_____

Address_____ ❑ Business or ❑ Home Address

Apt./Suite/Floor _____City _____State/Province_____

Zip/Postal Code_____Country _____

Phone (optional) _____E-mail (optional)_____

Limited time offer good for new subscribers in FT delivery areas only.
To order contact Financial Times Customer Service in your area (mention offer SAB01A).

The Americas: Tel 800-628-8088 Fax 845-566-8220 E-mail: uscirculation@ft.com

Europe: Tel 44 20 7873 4200 Fax 44 20 7873 3428 E-mail: fte.subs@ft.com

Japan: Tel 0120 341-468 Fax 0120 593-146 E-mail: circulation.fttokyo@ft.com

Korea: E-mail: sungho.yang@ft.com

S.E. Asia: Tel 852 2905 5555 Fax 852 2905 5590 E-mail: subseasia@ft.com

www.ft.com

FT FINANCIAL TIMES
World business newspaper

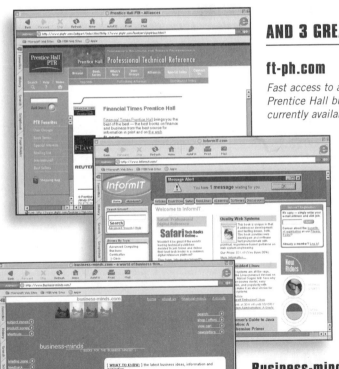